Advance Praise for *The Right—and Wrong—Stuff*

"Do your career a favor and read Carter Cast's new book. It's practical, thought-provoking, and funny—and it might just stop you from derailing when you least expect it."

— Dan Heath, coauthor of bestsellers *Made to Stick*, *Switch*, and *Decisive*

"Talent and drive aren't enough to prevent your career from derailing. After spending years exploring what causes people to stall or fall off the ladder, Carter Cast offers a book that's honest and actionable. Think of it as a mirror to help you see your blind spots."

— Adam Grant, *New York Times* bestselling author of *Give and Take*, *Originals*, and, with Sheryl Sandberg, *Option B*

"Carter Cast is a refreshingly original voice on a tough topic. His book will make you think differently about managing your career."

— Marshall Goldsmith, bestselling author of *What Got You Here Won't Get You There*

"Are you playing the right role at work? It may just be that the golden parts of your personality are precisely what are causing shadows to fall on your career. Carter Cast is a wise guide on how to get in sync with what the team around you is expecting from you."

— Seth Godin, bestselling author of *Tribes*

"Carter Cast breaks the mold for professors/practitioners with *The Right—and Wrong—Stuff*. The book reveals a unique set of five career archetypes that ring true, clear tips for accelerating your career, and page-turning stories of career success and failure."

—Dr. Geoff Smart, chairman and founder, ghSMART, and
New York Times bestselling author of *Who*

"This insightful and lively book is a pragmatic 'must-read' for all those aspiring to the C-suite. Cast brilliantly translates his grounded wisdom and classroom mastery onto the written page."

—Sally Blount, dean, Kellogg School of Management
at Northwestern University

"People tend to assume that careers are just about trajectory. They're really about knowing your strengths and weaknesses, then finding environments where you can adapt and flourish. Cast's insights are based on real-world experiences. This book will help so many people have the right career conversations to build their own Right Stuff."

—Gary Briggs, chief marketing officer, Facebook

"The most neglected fact in business is we're all human. Cast's brilliant, candid exploration of how self-awareness can make you a better leader should be required reading for managers at all levels of any organization. Know your blind spots and you'll have a very bright future."

—Chip Conley, hospitality entrepreneur and bestselling
author of *Emotional Equations*

"Cast's ability to demystify and shine a light on why talented people stumble is a gift to anyone trying to progress in their career. Cast's blend of no-nonsense, practical advice delivered with a good dose of humor makes *The Right—and Wrong—Stuff* a leadership book you'll actually enjoy reading while you are learning something."

—Laila Tarraf, former chief people officer, Peet's Coffee

"In *The Right—and Wrong—Stuff*, Cast offers an insightful exploration of the primary ways high-potential professionals can get off track in their careers and then provides a road map to success for those who are willing to put in the work. I highly recommend it to anyone who is serious about making the most of their career."

—Mike Gamson, senior vice president, Global Solutions, LinkedIn

"In *The Right—and Wrong—Stuff*, Cast has managed to combine a wealth of personal leadership experience in some of America's best-performing companies with some serious research into what makes for a successful career. Add a big dose of humility and humanity, and the result is a field guide to building your skills and leading your career that you need to have at arms-reach. It will become a dog-eared companion on your journey to career growth and well-being."

—**Brock Leach, former CEO, Tropicana and Frito-Lay North America**

"For anyone, at any level, who really wants to understand and traverse the 'leadership journey' (including the inevitable ups and downs), Cast delivers it in his first book in an honest, transparent manner. He is one of a very few practitioners and professors that can truly change your life. Knowing him has changed my life."

—**Harry Kraemer Jr., former chairman and CEO, Baxter International, Inc., and executive partner, Madison Dearborn Partners**

"In *The Right—and Wrong—Stuff*, Cast provides valuable insights for both individual career development and organizational effectiveness. His broad range of professional experiences, situational awareness, and interest in people and their development gives him a perceptive and unique perspective."

—**John Fleming, CEO, Global eCommerce, UNIQLO**

THE RIGHT—AND WRONG—STUFF

How Brilliant
Careers Are Made and Unmade

• • •

CARTER CAST

PUBLICAFFAIRS

New York

This book is dedicated to the memory of
Bradford Macomber.

PublicAffairs
Hachette Book Group
1290 Avenue of the Americas, New York, NY 10104
www.publicaffairsbooks.com
@Public_Affairs

Printed in the United States of America

First Edition: January 2018

Published by PublicAffairs, an imprint of Perseus Books, LLC, a
subsidiary of Hachette Book Group, Inc.

The publisher is not responsible for websites (or their content) that are
not owned by the publisher.

All illustrations © 2017 by Michael Meier

Library of Congress Cataloging in Publication Control
Number: 2017042061

ISBNs: 978-1-61039-709-4 (HC), 978-1-61039-710-0 (EB),
978-1-5417-6240-4 (INT'L)

LSC-C 10 9 8 7 6 5 4 3 2 1

CONTENTS

MY BLIND SPOT AND ITS TRAP DOOR

Most people think they know what they're good at. They are usually wrong.

Peter Drucker

I had just gotten off a phone call with Randy, a colleague with whom I had worked some twenty years ago. I hadn't spoken with him in years and, although it was great catching up, the thought that went through my mind that summer day in 2014 was "what happened?" Randy was smart, hardworking, well educated, and, after working for several strong, brand-name companies, had an admirable set of skills. He seemed to have "the right stuff." Yet his career had stalled somewhere along the way, and I could hear the disappointment in his voice when he talked about it. What went wrong?

That conversation led me to think back to one of those never-to-be-forgotten moments that we all experience: receiving bad career news. Mine took place in the mid-1990s, during a wilting performance review, where my boss described me as "obsti-nate," "resistant," and "insubordinate."

I was then a thirty-two-year-old marketer in PepsiCo's Frito-Lay division in Dallas. Up until that time, I'd had a pretty good nine-year run at PepsiCo, starting off in Wichita in 1986, as an assistant marketing manager for the Pizza Hut division, then, three years later, I became a marketing manager working on the initial expansion of the Taco Bell franchise into the Ontario, Canada, market. By 1995, I was a senior product manager, working in the new products department at Frito-Lay. I'd been fortunate enough to have received several promotions in my career at PepsiCo and was told that I had senior management potential. I had developed a skill set in the fundamentals of consumer marketing and could drive results by gaining the enlistment of others, because I was empathetic and had pretty good listening skills. I didn't feel compelled to take all the credit for accomplished work and, by and large, approached my job with a high degree of enthusiasm and a strong dose of irreverent humor. If asked, my peers probably would have said I was a hardworking, well-organized team player who was fun to work with. I was a big believer in one of Harry Truman's adages: "It's amazing what you can accomplish if you don't care who gets the credit."

Now I was sitting in my boss's office for my annual performance review. I worried as he started the preamble, a variation of the "this is going to hurt me more than it hurts you" theme. Smelling a rat, I flipped to the back page of my review, the "money page" in PepsiCo's review process. It gauged an employee's future potential with a job seniority level in the top right-hand corner of the page. Unlike in past reviews, where I'd seen "L18+" (level 18 is a senior vice president; at that time, I was a level 13, a senior manager), now I read the ominous words "Hold in Place." My ears started burning and I began to feel a strange sense of displacement, like I was out of my body, watching myself perform in a movie. I turned back to the first page of the review and tried to concentrate on what Mike, my boss, was saying to me.

Mike didn't bury the lead for long—he came right out and told me that I was considered, by senior management, to be unpromotable and was no longer on the fast track at Frito-Lay. He laid out a list of my offenses, littering his examples with words like "uncooperative," "resistant," and "unmanageable" as he described my behavior in various situations, such as the time he'd asked me to work alongside an outside consultant he'd hired for assistance on a marketplace analysis to determine the size and potential of the snack market for kids. Thinking it was part of my job to do this analysis, I ignored the consultant's requests to meet with me—a big mistake, as I was now coming to see.

Thirty painful minutes later, as he was wrapping up, Mike asked if I had anything to say for myself. I could tell he was frustrated, so I refrained from trying to defend myself. I could have told him that his insisting that I work with the consultant made me feel he lacked confidence in my abilities. I could have vented about how frustrated I'd become working within a large, matrixed organization, where decision making was slow and the approval rights unclear, and where I spent more time running the internal gauntlet to get projects approved than I did facing outward and developing new products and services that would appeal to our customers. Instead, I simply asked if I was being fired. He said, "No, but since we're going into the holiday break, I want you to take the next two weeks off and consider—really consider—if you want to be here. I'm not sure you do, to be honest. If you decide you want to stay here at Frito-Lay, I don't want you to work in my group any longer. You'll need to look for another marketing position within the company."

Over the break, I spoke with my parents about my predicament. At first, my thinking was that I didn't want to return—although

Frito-Lay is an excellent company, it just didn't feel like the right fit for me. During the past few years, as I'd moved into middle management, I'd become increasingly frustrated by the amount of time I spent on process management and the amount of effort I had to put into "greasing the skids"—trying to influence and cater to the various power players throughout the organization. I didn't think I had the right disposition for it. I became visibly impatient with and frustrated by the corporate bureaucracy. Although I was a good team player with my peers, when I felt the heavy hand of authority upon me, I wasn't. I tended to try to brush that heavy hand aside, to my own detriment. Two of my signature strengths— my self-starting nature and my sense of humor—had a destructive flip side. When feeling trod upon by "the man," I either ignored him or became irreverent, passive-aggressively expressing myself through ill-timed barbs of humor.

Although I felt it was time to leave the company, I didn't want to depart on such a bad note. When I asked my dad for advice, he said he was amazed that I'd lasted as long as I had inside a large organization. "You're a Cast," he said. "We tend to have trouble working in bureaucratic environments." My father worked independently—as a doctor who built his own surgical center—as did my grandfather, who was a free-ranging insurance salesman. I thought to myself, "You tell me that *now*, Dad, after nearly a decade working for corporations?!"

That event at Frito-Lay was an "aha moment" for me: Success, I started to understand, wasn't just about working hard and having a skill advantage, being industry-savvy and highly motivated. Even smart and talented people display behavioral problems that can stall their careers. My humiliating performance review stayed with me, and, as I've watched others go through career jags, getting demoted or fired, I eventually felt compelled to conduct research to discover the answer to these questions: *What really impedes the career progress of talented people? Why do some careers stall while others flourish?*

I found that many of us are closer to career derailment than we might think. Because bosses often provide little more than sporadic (at best) and nonspecific performance feedback (in hindsight I am thankful that Mike's feedback to me that day was crystal clear), it's common that we aren't made aware of a performance issue until it's too late. The fact is that one-half to two-thirds of managers and leaders will experience career derailment. At some point, over *half of us* will get fired or demoted—or our careers will flatline and we won't reach our innate potential. And I found that there are five common reasons why it happens, which I've expressed through archetypes—characterizations that demonstrate, in a microcosm, how and why talented people experience career derailment. I've done this to humanize this uncomfortable topic. If your first reaction is "none of these characters is like me," look past their specific characterizations and into their behavioral tendencies—chances are you will find a few gold nuggets that you can address to improve your performance. For example, although I've never been told I was "sharp-elbowed" or an "egomaniac" like the first archetype, Captain Fantastic, there are aspects of him in me. The truth is I derailed because I was dismissive of my boss's input and acted arrogantly.

The Five Archetypes

Captain Fantastic

These are the folks whose sharp elbows bruise you on their quest for the Holy Grail of the corner office. They suffer from interpersonal issues because of unbridled ego drive and dismal listening skills, resulting in poor working relationships with coworkers. Captain Fantastics, with their mantra of "I-me-mine" may initially rise up through the organization, but, because they alienate others, when they're placed in broader and more complex roles that require the support of others, more often than not, like Icarus, they flame out.

The Solo Flier

Often these are strong individual contributors who are very good at executing their initiatives—Solo Fliers not only deliver the bacon, they cut and wrap it as well. They are self-starting, self-contained, multitalented achievement dynamos. But when they get promoted into managerial positions, they have difficulty building and leading teams and revert to either micromanaging or trying to do the work themselves. Their teams become dissatisfied and eventually there's a *coup d'état*. The way they operate can be summed up when they communicate to others, either verbally or nonverbally: "step aside, I've got this."

Version 1.0

These people, comfortable in their routines, are highly skeptical of change. They resist learning new skills that would help them adapt to the rapidly changing business environment. They resist using new technologies that could help them perform their jobs better and faster. When new management comes into their company to shake things up, they often form part of a rear guard resisting change. They may call themselves "traditionalists," but in reality they are overly cautious. Their attitude of "if it ain't broke, don't fix it" will not serve them well over time, and eventually their dinosaur-like tendencies may lead to extinction.

The One-Trick Pony

These folks are good at doing a good job at what they're good at. The problem is they become so reliant on what they're good at—a signature skill—that, over time, unbeknownst to them, they become one-dimensional and unpromotable. Whereas Version 1.0s resist change, One-Trick Ponies don't realize they need to change—that they've overspecialized and have become pigeon-holed into doing one thing for their firm. Their upward mobility stops because they've done the same thing over and over and haven't had a diverse set of work experiences that provide them with a broad strategic perspective. They don't understand how other departments function and don't grasp the activities that drive value for their company's business. They thought their belief that "we live in an age of specialization" led them to take the right approach, but they came to realize that their careers are now limited because of their narrowness.

The Whirling Dervish

These people run around the office like their hair is on fire, late for the next meeting and muttering to themselves about their workload. They lack planning and organizational skills; they're often creative people with a host of ideas spewing out of their brains like a hyperactive geyser—but they have a hard time converting their ideas into action. Because they are known to overcommit and underdeliver, their boss and coworkers can't count on them to complete their assigned tasks, and eventually people try to avoid working with them. Whirling Dervishes don't deliver on promises, wondering, "where did the time go?!"

Necessary Conversations Aren't Occurring

People with these traits are in every organization—from big corporations to small law firms, from educational institutions to early stage start-ups. These five archetypes cut across not only type and stage of organization, but also gender and level of seniority. As it turns out, the research on which these archetypes are based is robust and consistent. So, an important and puzzling question is: Why aren't companies doing a better job of helping their employees identify and address these five common behavioral issues in order to reduce the rate of worker derailment? *Why isn't the topic of derailment included as part of career development conversations?* The answer, to a certain extent, lies in the popularity of the "focusing on your strengths" movement. Without a doubt, the "strengths movement" is a positive development. What's not to like about a philosophy that focuses on our upside—one based on the premise that we're happier and perform better when we understand what we're good at and put ourselves into jobs that leverage those strengths? The problem comes when it's taken too far and used to the exclusion of other methods of self-examination and career development. "Accentuate the positive" has become a new mantra in many workplaces, where, according to the *Wall Street Journal*, "bosses now dole out frequent praise, urge employees to celebrate small victories and focus performance reviews around a particular worker's strengths—instead of dwelling on why he flubbed a client presentation."

There are two problems with companies' excessive focus on the positive. First, not all strengths are of equal importance. What you're good at might not be what your firm needs you to be good at. The value placed on particular strengths often depends on the job context; the strengths needed usually vary by industry type, by job function, and by firm size and stage of development. You may have a set of skills or several strong behavioral traits that just aren't of primary importance for your company at its particular state of incarnation. For example, you may be an empathetic person with excellent account management skills but that may not be of primary importance if you're at an early stage venture that needs you to have outstanding selling skills to bring in new accounts.

Second and more damaging is that the overreliance on "focusing on your strengths" can mask a critical skill gap or a personal blind spot that stops a talented person's career in its tracks. The derailment research shows that careers stall more from having the "wrong stuff" (e.g., being insensitive to others) than lacking the "right stuff" (e.g., not having strong analytical skills). Competency assessments are widely used to gauge personal traits such as mental horsepower, emotional intelligence, and decisiveness as well as job skills, such as technical know-how. The problem is, these assessments gauge the "right stuff" areas and do not examine the "wrong stuff" areas, where people are vulnerable to derailment. The reason boils down to a preference for focusing on the positive—competency development—and not addressing the negative—fixing issues that may lead to derailment. But without having these necessary hard conversations, people suffer because they're left unaware of a blind spot or area of vulnerability instead of being able to develop a plan to resolve or mitigate it. *As a result, people are not receiving the personal feedback they need to improve, and their careers are suffering.* Organizations pursuing a developmental strategy focusing on strengths alone will not lead to the career ascension of their employees. Sooner or later, unaddressed developmental needs will limit the career progress of good people.

*

After talking to my parents and several friends and mentors and going through a decent amount of self-reflection, I decided to return to Frito-Lay. I wanted to redeem myself and also to avoid a black mark on my résumé. I was able to find work in another group, but it wasn't easy. As I peddled my wares, I found out I'd developed a reputation with senior management for being difficult to manage. I ended up working for Stephen Quinn, who had just moved to the United States from our Canadian division. He wasn't fully aware of my problem-child reputation, and I was thankful that he took me into his group.

After rereading my performance review and reflecting on what my now former boss Mike had told me, I realized that I needed to understand the circumstances that triggered my bad behavior and to develop practical methods to better self-regulate and curb my tendency toward insubordination. First, I looked back on all the core activities I performed in my last assignment and wrote down the situations where I became frustrated and my rebellious tendency was activated. It seemed to come out in ponderous process-oriented meetings, especially when the conversation turned to matters related to turf and power, such as departmental approval rights, or when the conversation turned to mind-numbing internal procedural steps that needed to be taken to give a project the green light. It also seemed to rear its ugly head when I was told what to do by an authority figure for whom I lacked professional regard, such as the vice president of packaging, who, in an effort to reduce the level of complexity for his team, lobbied for me to cut the "hot salsa" item from our Tostitos lineup, not understanding that it would reduce our retail shelf space in the grocery aisle and cut the sales rate across our entire product line.

After listing a handful of these "charged" circumstances where my bad behavior popped out, I realized I needed some kind of reminder—a device to help me maintain self-awareness and to self-monitor in situations that played to my areas of vulnerability. So I did two things. First, I created a screen saver on my desktop computer that said "Roark." Howard Roark, the unflappable protagonist in Ayn Rand's book *The Fountainhead*, handled the slings and arrows of outrageous fortune with aplomb. Like Ronald Reagan, the arrows bounced off Roark. He had rhino hide. I, too, needed to learn to depersonalize business feedback that came my way. Second, I found a thick rubber band and wrote "B" on

it in several places. When I found myself in a glacially slow process meeting, exasperated enough to let out a little verbal steam,
I looked down at that rubber band and remembered to simply
breathe. Breathe slowly from my diaphragm and watch the urge
to vent just pass, preventing me from saying something I might
regret.

I still remember one case in particular where this simple practice served me well. I was in a product review meeting for Tostitos, the brand on which I worked. All the muckety-mucks were in
attendance—everyone from the CEO to the head of manufacturing to the chief marketing officer. I arrived early and quietly took a
seat at the large boardroom table. Eventually, the room filled. My
boss, a vice president of marketing, was standing at the front of the
room, ready to kick off the session. Then, a big cheese, the head
of R&D entered the room, late, walked up to me and stated quite
loudly, "You're sitting in my chair." A question formed in my head:
"Oh, is this the director's chair? Is your name on the back of it, like
a Spielberg or Scorsese?" Instead, I looked down, saw the "B" on
the rubber band, and took a deep breath. Then I said, "Excuse me"
and found a seat on the perimeter of the room. Prior to my poor
performance review, the chances are good I would have delivered
a useless and destructive retort to the head of R&D. Now I just got
up and moved.

Over time, I was again considered to be a promotable employee,
and I was eventually moved up from a manager to a director role,
in no small part due to the counsel and support of my new boss,
Stephen Quinn. He counseled me on how to deal with senior management, and he took the time to work with me on my particular
area of personal vulnerability. That area was (and still is) an interpersonal issue that manifests itself in the form of a self-defeating
behavior that one leadership expert, Robert Hogan, calls being
"mischievous"—someone who seeks excitement, likes to test limits,

wants immediate results, and doesn't do routines well. According to Hogan's research, there are eleven common "dark side" personality tendencies that pop out, often under pressure, and hurt us. Hogan found that a staggering 98 percent of people have at least one of these eleven tendencies. I had run headlong into a manifestation of the most common and most damaging career derailer: suffering from *interpersonal issues*; in my case, this "dark side" tendency of being mischievous popped out when I was provoked by either corporate bureaucracy or heavy-handed authority figures.

Twenty years after that performance review, through LinkedIn, I located Mike—the boss who'd delivered the tough message—and asked if we could talk. I hadn't spoken to him since the mid-1990s. On a phone call, I asked if he remembered that review. Mike chuckled and said, "Oh, yes," and went on to say,

> With your review I was pretty matter of fact. We were trying to create a new vision in my group and I didn't see you as engaged in it. You weren't doing what I wanted you to do—instead you did what you wanted. You were this smart and charming guy who realized he could get what he wanted by being smart and charming and I wanted you to do something more. I wanted you to use your skills of persuasion to help lead *my* agenda. But you didn't want to do that. So you needed to hear that message. If you wanted to stay at the company, you had to do things differently.

Back in the 1990s, senior executives at PepsiCo used an analogy that Mike cited, saying that our senior managers and leaders were "eagles who fly in formation." I remember that analogy used to make me grimace. To me it felt demotivating and restrictive. But it became clear to me after Mike's review that if I wanted to dig out of my hole and remain employed at PepsiCo, I had to embrace this philosophy to some extent and learn to fly straight, in formation, and not veer off the prescribed path.

Even though many years have passed since my Frito-Lay days, as I listened to Mike describe his experience working with me back then, I still cringed when he said, for emphasis, the repetitive and sardonic line about my being "smart and charming." I lacked self-awareness back then—I didn't understand the destructive effects that my propensity to be mischievous had on my career until I received a gut punch and derailed. But, in hindsight, Mike's performance review was the most useful I've ever received—surely more helpful than a glowing one. His honest assessment allowed me to better understand my own vulnerabilities and forced me to face and mitigate them in order to progress in my career.

What Exactly Is Derailment?

Derailment occurs when a manager or an executive previously deemed to have strong potential is fired, demoted, or plateaus below his or her expected levels of performance. It's the result, two leadership researchers found, of "a lack of fit between individual values and development, on the one hand, and organizational values and needs, on the other." The reasons for derailment, then, extend beyond job-specific issues, such as a skill gap or lack of experiential knowledge, and even beyond interpersonal issues that impede one's ability to manage or lead. Derailment may be the result of a lack of cultural fit between the values and motives of the individual and those of the firm itself. That was certainly the case with me. Although I did suffer from an interpersonal issue (my tendency toward insubordination in certain circumstances), it was further provoked by my having values and needs that weren't well aligned with the cultural norms at Frito-Lay. I valued autonomy and creativity, I was not motivated by power, and I was demotivated by procedure. Years later, I took the Hogan personality tests and the assessment was that I valued "independent self-expression, innovation and unconventional thought," was "suspicious of conventional beliefs," and disliked environments that were "old-fashioned or conservative and emphasize procedures over understanding." The assessment said I should seek work environments that "value creativity, imagination, emphasize the quality of product design and tolerate eccentricity." Frito-Lay, although an outstanding company, did not fit that bill in 1995. My problem was that I didn't know this about myself at the time.

Often, prior to failing, people who derail were successful and considered talented up-and-comers. Derailment often afflicts talented managers who are either unaware of a debilitating weakness or interpersonal blind spot or arrogant enough to believe that developmental feedback doesn't apply to them. Talented managers and leaders, as we will see time and again in the stories that follow, are often "knocked off the fast track" due to a lack of self-awareness around an interpersonal issue or a key skill gap and an unwillingness, once confronted with it, to adjust their behavior accordingly. It is often hubris—not lack of talent—that causes people on the rise to fall.

Getting things done through others—the essence of leadership—requires a combination of technical skills (being proficient in areas important to the success of the business), intrapersonal skills (especially strong self-management skills, which are driven by self-understanding and self-control), and interpersonal skills (the ability to develop and foster strong relationships and gain the enlistment of others). People may derail due to a lack of technical, job-related skills, but more common reasons have to do with intrapersonal or interpersonal issues that impede them from enlisting people to accomplish goals. A revealing part of my research included conducting a survey of one hundred derailed managers and then executing follow-up interviews with a subset of the derailed population. My research found that "a lack of self-awareness" and "difficulty working with others" were the top two reasons that these one hundred people experienced a career derailment event. As the late, great management expert Peter Drucker said, as in the epigraph to this Introduction, "Most people think they know what they're good at. They are usually wrong." Or, as Robert Hogan, Joyce Hogan, and Robert Kaiser, three often-cited derailment researchers, write, "Derailment can almost always be traced to relationship problems."

There are of course times when people derail because of personal circumstances, such as health problems, or personal priorities, such as a reluctance to relocate or the desire to improve their work–life balance. Although these are critical aspects of a person's career equation, they are of a personal nature and highly individualized and hard to address and generalize at a macro level. Because of that, my focus in this book will be primarily on derailment as it occurs inside the walls of the office.

My Purpose

I want to shine a light on this buried topic of derailment in order to help talented people realize their potential. My goal is to help you understand, assess, and correct problems that could otherwise stall your career. I will discuss a variety of strategies to help you avoid derailment or get back on track when derailment occurs, focusing in particular on three key remedies:

- *Becoming more aware of your own areas of vulnerability,* especially potential interpersonal issues;
- *Understanding new job requirements* during times of change and transition; and
- *Increasing your learning agility* to become more "career flexible" and taking charge of your own career development.

You will find advice from experts and many actual stories of talented people who stumbled in their careers but got back on track and how they did it. You will also find self-assessment questions to help you identify your own derailment propensities, which I developed and tested with MBA and executive students at the Kellogg School of Management. And you will find a host of practical remedies to address any derailment propensities that you realize you have.

In Part One of the book, I examine, in detail, each of the five major reasons for career derailment and lay out corrective measures.

In Part Two, I examine the behavior of high performers, juxtaposing what these people with "the right stuff" do to distinguish themselves from average or below-average performers. I examine their traits, behaviors, and growth practices, discussing why they are viewed favorably and have strong career momentum.

Then, in an effort to help ensure you're in the right job—that you have the right career "fit"—I close by examining ways to improve your self-understanding, digging into the topic of motives, and then I finish by laying out eight ways to take charge of your own career.

A friend of mine who is an executive coach calls derailers "blind spots with trap doors." Our blind spot doesn't allow us to see an area of personal vulnerability until we've already dropped through the floor. Although these derailers often surprise us, they don't surprise those around us. Ironically, they're often blind spots in clear sight. The goal of this book is to make these blind spots visible to you, to shine a light on them so you can take corrective action and navigate around those trap doors and continue to progress in your career.

PART ONE

THE FIVE ARCHETYPES

CHAPTER 1

CAPTAIN FANTASTIC

Human Wrecking Balls Who Wreck Themselves

C aptain Fantastic bursts into your office without knocking, interrupting a meeting you're having with Bill, one of the people on your team. The Captain says, "Sorry, but we gotta talk. Only take a minute." He is the vice president of merchandising and you are a marketing manager, so you reluctantly comply, saying, "OK, Bill and I are just about finished here. Give me two minutes." "Sorry," he says, "but we need to talk *now*! I'm hopping on the Gulfstream in an hour with the chief."

Without waiting for an answer or for Bill to leave, he plops down in a chair and launches into an account of how your marketing campaign for *his* new line of glitter blue jeans is ineffective. "The models aren't hot; the copy is pedestrian at best—the word play on 'glitter and Twitter' is lame. And I have yet to see any of the ads on prime-time programming—where are they running, on late-night TV, alongside the Chia Pet ads?"

You take a deep breath, prepared to address each of his concerns. But as you begin to explain that these natural-looking models scored higher in concept appeal tests with your customers than any of the heroin-chic models your competitors were using, he interrupts, saying, "Look, I'm giving you the courtesy of this meeting. Just so you know, I'm gonna have to get this campaign pulled off the air, and I'm recommending that we use a different ad agency. I know a group who does good work." When you remind him that advertising decisions are under the discretion of the marketing department, not merchandising, he says, "Not when it's not selling product." Then he up and leaves.

With the deft touch of a sledgehammer, Captain Fantastic leaves a trail of carnage on his drive for the corner office. At his worst, he's a human wrecking ball known for being insensitive, arrogant, and emotionally volatile. Dismissive of input or advice from anyone else, he has few friends to help him when the tide turns and business results soften, which they inevitably do. When the results are strong, decision makers often look the other way or forgive Captain Fantastic. But when performance weakens, the Captain Fantastics of the world get fired.

Where They Go Wrong

Captain Fantastic is a characterization or archetype of the way people can suffer from the damaging effects of their interpersonal behavior. The Captain's poor ego management results in behavior that is a combination of arrogance (in particular, insensitivity, aloofness, and dismissiveness) and defensiveness (especially not being open to criticism and having poor listening skills). Fueling the Captain's poor ego management is his nearly laughable (but not if you're at the receiving end of his tirades) lack of self-awareness, particularly his inability to understand how his words and actions affect others.

People who suffer from the Captain Fantastic syndrome may end up flaming out due to:

- Arrogance, especially being dismissive of others' input;
- Excessive ambition, focusing on their own career at the expense of others;
- Being defensive, especially having poor listening skills and not being open to constructive criticism;
- Being insensitive and lacking empathy for others' feelings;
- Lacking composure and having poor stress management skills, including outbursts and overreacting; and
- Being distrustful of others' intentions.

People with poor interpersonal skills suffer from the fallout of what certainly is "the great derailer." Marshall Goldsmith, a prominent executive coach and the author of *What Got You Here Won't Get You There* believes that "the single biggest career derailer I see is lack of ego management—lack of humility, lack of willingness to shut up and listen and learn."

The Captain Fantastic syndrome is in fact the number one reason why people run into career trouble—regardless of age, salary level, ethnicity, or gender. If anything, the need to develop strong interpersonal relations becomes even more pronounced as we progress in our careers. As people move from individual contributor to manager and into larger leadership positions, they increasingly rely on others to complete ever-more-complex work projects. As I have said more than once to talented up-and-comers who have a touch of arrogance and have yet to realize the benefits of taking the time to establish strong interpersonal working relationships, "Remember: 'We' knows more than 'me.'" Stuart Kaplan, the director of leadership recruiting at Google, reinforced this point during a conversation with me: "As you progress [in your career], your relationship with others is more important than your knowledge of and relationship with data. This need kicks in as you move into middle and upper management. It's a mind-set change." He continued, "You have to suppress your ego, let go of having the answer, and embrace the relational world. It becomes less about having competencies and more about engendering trust."

Jana Rich, a highly respected executive recruiter in Silicon Valley and founder of the Rich Talent Group who has placed executives at companies such as Airbnb, Google, and Uber, stressed how poor ego management and, correspondingly, poor listening skills can thwart people during a job interview. "When I interview a candidate, I always ask this one question: 'Will you please give me a ten-minute walk through your career, focusing on the how and why of your career transitions? I've read your bio and résumé, so I'm not looking for what you did in each job and your accomplishments. I'm interested in how you thought through your transitions. Again, please keep your answer to ten minutes.'" Then Jana laughed and continued: "I'm not joking—you would not believe how frequently I get these long, rambling thirty- to forty-minute answers! Where is their self-awareness? Where are their listening skills? What about their engagement skills? Where's that give and take that creates an interesting conversation? Is it only about them and their agenda? When job candidates go on and on after I asked for brevity, I worry about their interpersonal sensitivity, not being other-oriented, not being able to bring others along with them."

There are a handful of interpersonal behaviors that commonly lead people toward derailment. Six of the worst offenders are defensiveness, arrogance, lack of composure, being distrustful, being mischievous and colorful, and being passive.

Defensive people face the danger of having an inaccurate view of their own performance. Peers and subordinates tend to shy away from offering their perspectives (why bother?—their thoughts will be dismissed immediately). Eventually defensive people find that they aren't receiving accurate, helpful feedback on their work. This can be an enormous issue over time and can lead to derailment. People who are defensive and fail to give criticism due consideration don't learn from experience and stop improving. Early in my career, I struggled with being defensive when encountering critical feedback—and lacked self-awareness about this trait. Instead of looking for the pearl inside the comment, I'd busy myself with conjuring a justifiable comeback remark. And the likelihood of my being defensive was directly proportional to the amount of time and effort I put into a project. As a young marketing manager for Taco Bell Canada, I was very excited about presenting our new TV advertising campaign to our division's vice president of marketing. But as he noticed flaws and picked it apart, I found myself interrupting him time and again to justify what I felt was a very creative new campaign. Eventually he said, "You sound like a frog, Carter. 'Yeah-but,' 'Yeah-but,' 'Yeah-but.' Why don't you stop croaking and start listening? I've been doing restaurant marketing for quite some time."

To counter this tendency, I created a mantra that I use when encountering critical feedback: "I shift into neutral; I shift into neutral; I shift into neutral . . ." I am certainly not alone in having this trait. You can find evidence of people suffering from defensiveness just about everywhere. I recently opened my newspaper to the sports section, where I read that former Philadelphia 76er superstar Allen Iverson was elected into the NBA Basketball Hall of Fame. Iverson said he hadn't called his coach, Larry Brown, to thank him yet, because he thought he'd "cry like a baby" when he heard Brown's voice. "I love being who I am," Iverson told reporters following the introduction ceremony of the 2016 class. "I feel comfortable in my skin. But if I could have a wish, as an athlete,

I wish I would have bought into what he [Coach Larry Brown] was trying to give me all along. Just being defiant, being a certified a**hole for nothing—when all he wanted was the best for me. . . . I didn't take constructive criticism the way I should have." Iverson goes on to say that once he stopped rebelling and started listening to Coach Brown, he went from being just a talented player to the league's MVP, and his team reached the NBA finals.

Captain Fantastic has the interpersonal defect of *arrogance* in spades. Like the Captain, arrogant people often rise quickly through the ranks of an organization due to their boldness but then have a spectacular fall. They are often self-absorbed and focused on their upward career trajectory, but at the expense of others and what's good for the team. They may "manage up" well, but not sideways with peers and downward with those at lower levels. I saw many examples of this at PepsiCo: a smart, well-educated, very ambitious guy would go rocketing up the organization. Eventually he would assume a broad, complex leadership position, where he needed to rely on others to get work done, and, believing he had all the answers, he would be dismissive of others' input. No one would want to work for or with him—he would not be able to gain others' enlistment in order to successfully deliver against his accountabilities. Then, at a later date, I'd read an announcement from HR that this Captain Fantastic "is moving onto a special project," and twelve weeks later he'd be gone.

"When I think about what throws a person's career offtrack," noted Raul Vazquez, the CEO of Oportun, a company that provides credit-establishing, affordable loans to people without credit scores, "I think of ego in particular. When ego needs overwhelm a person's natural pride for their work, they run into trouble. It becomes a battle between self and others. To what extent are you motivated by doing things for yourself versus serving the needs of the team?" Raul recalled a "very talented up-and-coming young marketer who tried to push his massive agenda onto his peers. He wasn't interested in listening to their rational objections; he just kept cramming his agenda down others' throats. He was smart and very skilled. But his ambition wasn't balanced with prudence or empathy for others' perspectives. He just pressed forward and asked for forgiveness later. He'd do it his way and say 'sorry' later. His actions came at the expense of others." Raul paused and then said, "He didn't last at the company."

A third interpersonal issue that derails workers is being volatile and overly excitable. *Lacking composure* makes it particularly hard for managers to be effective with their subordinates. Team members look to their leaders for stability, optimism, and hope. Having an erratic boss who responds poorly to stress is very disconcerting. They wonder, "Who's going to show up?" Whereas arrogant people are going to act arrogantly and defensive people will act defensively, people who lack composure are wild cards. At their best, they're really good. Volatile, excitable people are often creative and committed. But, at their worst, they destabilize their group. Brooke Vuckovic, an executive coach and adjunct lecturer of leadership coaching at the Kellogg School of Management, said,

> The impact of a volatile leader radiates out. Their volatility is very hard for those around them. When junior employees act out, they get read the riot act—often immediately. But when more senior-level people are volatile, the system doesn't always respond—until it's too late. Here's why: volatile leaders often manage impressions extremely well with those who have the power in their organizations, or, they are so valuable that people don't want to risk alienating them by giving them feedback. This derailer demands an unusual (and unfair) level of composure from the people they lead, who must maintain their composure when their leader can't.

Or they are left having to smooth the waters their bosses have churned. It's hard to manage through, and can create a dysfunctional working environment for the entire team.

A fourth interpersonal issue that hurts the career of talented people is being *mischievous and overly dramatic*. Given their lack of impulse control, these colorful people can be dangerous to put in front of senior management or important customers for fear of their saying the wrong thing. People with this trait also tend to have difficulty maintaining focus on the task at hand or staying on course with key business priorities. Colorful, dramatic people are often imaginative—they are fascinated by new ideas but are susceptible to changing their direction on a whim. They can be distracted by "bright, shiny objects." When you talk to people who work for dramatic, limit-testing bosses, you'll hear that, at their best, they are creative, visionary, and inspiring but at their worst they are impulsive, attention-seeking, distractible people who don't manage their teams well and make poor business decisions. A 360-degree feedback report from a peer of a senior-level enterprise software sales manager who suffered from being impulsive and colorful noted that "he has way too many 'look at me' moments, especially when he has an audience of underlings—or when we're on a road trip, recruiting for new talent. It's like someone winds him up and he just goes off. Stories. Jokes. Tall tales. It can be funny but then he overplays it. He'd probably tell you that he's warming up the room, but beneath his stories, it's all about him. And it's terribly distracting. We waste time. It takes us from our task at hand."

Regarding the fifth interpersonal issue, people who are *distrustful* can be hard workers with high performance standards. Their watchful skepticism can yield accurate insights about political machinations inside their company. But they can also be pessimistic and difficult to work with. Subordinates often find them to be micromanagers and poor delegators. Peers often find that their excessive skepticism and distrust brings work projects to a crawl as suspicion strains relationships and creates antagonism. A group of us at PepsiCo dubbed these folks "the sales prevention society," and, when working on cross functional initiatives, we tried our best to keep them from being assigned to our projects. I've found this trait of playing the skeptic to be a natural tendency for people working in technical functions (like manufacturing, research and development, or software development) and in finance and legal. Although it's understandable and often appropriate—the very nature of these jobs is to be rigorous, exacting, and careful in order to develop and protect the assets of the company—I've had many experiences, particularly with corporate legal counsel or with finance managers and CFOs, where their protective skepticism crossed over the line of prudence and into a distrust for "the new." In these encounters, I've tried to reframe the conversation from "why we can't" to "how we can."

When it comes to the sixth interpersonal derailment tendency, *passive* people, at their best, are "good soldiers" who steadily advance their projects. At their worst they clog organizations, slowing innovation and creating a culture of mediocrity. Their risk aversion and inability to act independently ensures nothing remarkable is accomplished. Ted Martin, an executive recruiter who places senior-level executives into high-growth venture capital and private equity companies, said,

In my line of business, I interview plenty of people who talk a lot about how busy they are, how full their plates are and they translate that into being a hard worker who deserves more responsibility. But be careful. Just because you show up on time for every meeting, follow directions and do your part doesn't mean you're a high performer or should get promoted. There are plenty of people out there who fall into a bucket I call "process facilitators." They move things along on the proverbial assembly line but they don't drive organizational change. They're in a very different category than the high performers who bust out and create something that wasn't there before.

Of these six interpersonal issues, I would call out the dangers of *defensiveness* because it suppresses the ability to learn and develop. Self-understanding is a key component of career success and defensiveness reduces the ability to examine and adjust behavior. Research indicates that defensive people receive less feedback than open-minded people. Their perception becomes increasingly inaccurate and their blind spots multiply.

The problems associated with not being aware of one's interpersonal issues can be seen with twenty-seven-year-old Cecilia Brooks, who went through a management development program in store operations at one of the largest retailers in the United States. Bright and motivated, she performed well in her training assignments. After eighteen months of training, Cecilia was promoted to a human resources job at a different retail store within the company, where she oversaw the staffing of new positions and managed the orientation of newly hired people. "It was," she said, "a big store, and I was the number two HR person there." But a year later she left because, as she put it, "I wanted a break from retail." When I gently dug a little deeper, other reasons became apparent. "Well," she said, "there weren't really the growth opportunities I thought there'd be. It didn't really look like I'd be able to get the next job." When I asked her if there was any particular feedback she'd heard about her performance that might explain the lack of available growth opportunities, she said, "Yes, there was one thing. I got feedback that I was too forceful and aggressive in team meetings and when I met with my peers. Turnover was an issue at this store and I was under a lot of pressure to fix it. In my first meeting at the new store, I came in with this great plan—really well thought out—on how to fix it. What everybody needed to do to fix it. It was a really good plan. And they were like, 'Hey, we don't even know you. Slow down.'" When I asked if this was an isolated occasion, she said, "I guess not. We had these quarterly review meetings and I heard from my boss that I didn't get buy-in from people before I recommended a plan. I guess I heard that a lot, really. I think my boss felt like I wasn't taking in that feedback." "Were you?" I asked. "I think so, but I kept getting new bosses," Cecilia replied. "That was frustrating." When I asked if she heard similar feedback from the new boss, Cecilia said, "I guess so, yes. I think I find it hard to hear criticism. I'm a perfectionist and take bad feedback really hard. I don't like it. I deny it. I only like hearing good things."

A Walk on the Dark Side

What often lurks behind these six interpersonal issues are aberrant personality dimensions that often come to light during times of stress, as when Cecilia rotated to a new store and was tasked with fixing the employee turnover problem. Six decades ago, psychoanalyst Karen Horney developed an influential theory around neuroses and the dark side of personality that is still used today. Horney's clinical research with patients led her to believe that a neurosis is simply how people address and manage through interpersonal issues that they encounter on a daily basis. She viewed neuroses as our ongoing coping mechanisms and identified three broad categories of coping strategies based on these needs: "moving against people," "moving away from people," and "moving toward people."

According to Horney, with *"moving against people,"* we desire control by seeking power and social recognition. We attempt to accomplish this by reverting to aggressive behavior or through charm or manipulation. We behave like this as a defensive strategy to protect ourselves from others taking advantage of us and to reinforce our worth as a person. This is the primary coping strategy of Captain Fantastic. Beneath his bluster is very likely a frightened boy who feels the needs to "move against people before they move against him."

With *"moving away from people"* the coping theme is managing one's insecurities through avoidance or detachment, manifested in the desire for self-sufficiency and autonomy in order to protect oneself. The need to be above reproach—for perfection—is another defining trait of this coping strategy. Receiving criticism and being flawed is unacceptable and will denigrate our self-worth so we check and recheck our work, polish and repolish it in hopes of avoiding criticism. Or we simply opt out and don't engage for fear of being criticized or "found out"—we stay on the sidelines, away from center stage.

Last, in *"moving toward people"* the coping theme is managing insecurities through compliance, seen in seeking affection and approval and ingratiating ourselves with others. At work we are dutiful and eager to please. We avoid confrontation at all cost.

In the 1990s, two psychologists, Robert and Joyce Hogan, built on Horney's work and developed a personality assessment tool, the Hogan Development Survey, which is used in business by many career coaches to help identify personality-based performance risks that stem from interpersonal behavior problems. This survey instrument assesses and scores people on eleven "dark side" personality dimensions that Hogan grouped under Horney's three coping strategies. These dimensions are behaviors, derived from years of research, that can damage working relationships and reduce productivity and, if not addressed, can limit overall career potential or lead to derailment. I have summarized the Hogan "dark side" dimensions and their relation to Horney's work below.

Hogan's research indicates that nearly all of us have at least one "dark side" personality trait and that most people have two or three. I recently took the Hogan Development Survey and it revealed my "mischievous" tendency as well as a "leisurely" one. I've written about the damaging effects of my predilection toward being "mischievous." My "leisurely" tendency, which Hogan describes as "stubborn, independent and cynical about the intentions of others, especially superiors," came in the form of pursuing my own agenda over my boss's. If I worked under someone I respected, I was hardworking and diligent—a model employee. I followed direction, turned in my work on time, and looked for opportunities to forward my boss's agenda. But if I found my boss to be extremely deliberate, overly cautious, or a micromanager, I eventually resisted taking direction. I did this by picking and choosing what I would focus on, not taking into account all

Hogan Dark Side Personality Dimensions

Horney Coping Strategy	Hogan Dark Side Personality Dimension
"Moving away" (cope through detachment)	**Excitable** (moody, volatile) **Skeptical** (distrustful) **Cautious** (resists change) **Reserved** (aloof, insensitive) **Leisurely** (passive resistance)
"Moving against" (cope through aggression or manipulation)	**Bold** (arrogant, entitled) **Mischievous** (charming, excitement-seeking) **Colorful** (melodramatic, attention-seeking) **Imaginative** (creative, eccentric)
"Moving toward" (cope by complying)	**Diligent** (precise, inflexible) **Dutiful** (eager to please)

my boss's requests. I discovered at Frito-Lay, when I embarrassed myself and was put in the penalty box for a couple years, that this wasn't a particularly effective managerial strategy. As the Bobby Fuller Four sang, "I fought the law and the law won." I took the Hogan assessment in 2014 when I was fifty-one. I wish I'd taken it much earlier in my career and had made it a priority to increase my self-understanding.

Psychologist Daniel Goleman's work on emotional intelligence reinforces the importance of understanding our own behavioral derailment tendencies so we can actively monitor and manage them. Goleman says two intrapersonal skills are critical to avoiding self-destructive tendencies: *self-awareness*, or having the ability to recognize and understand one's own moods, emotions, and drives and their effect on others; and *self-regulation*, or the ability to control or redirect disruptive impulses and moods and to think before acting upon them. If I would have taken the time to gain a better understanding of my behavioral vulnerabilities, I may well have developed effective self-monitoring tools and avoided that painful derailment event.

Alex Moy, a talented director of product management at Gogo, a provider of in-flight entertainment and information content, told me about feedback he'd received when he was at U.S. Cellular that helped him progress in his career:

> I grew up as an engineer, where people are generally very direct with each other. When I was promoted into management, I got very direct feedback about being a bull in a china shop, especially in important situations such as meetings about product where people tend to be very tense. A really good boss told me that I needed to slow down, spend more time listening before speaking, observe others—how they were behaving—and then figure out how to bring them along with me, how to position things to them versus being

so direct and confrontational. This feedback was a pivotal moment for me. My boss said he had suffered from the same tendency, so he was very credible to me.

Self-awareness and self-knowledge are critically important in reducing the chances of career derailment, as Laila Tarraf discovered. Now the director of human capital at private equity firm GI Partners, Laila previously was the first chief people officer at Peet's Coffee & Tea. By her own admission, she failed to make progress in her career when she was in her twenties due to a lack of discipline and focus and her blind spot of not understanding how she came across to others. She could be, she said, "impetuous, overly critical, and show a lack of respect when things moved along too slowly. That contributed to my not getting off the ground earlier in my career." When I asked Laila how she addressed this issue (clearly she eventually achieved liftoff, given the senior-level positions she has reached), she said that one of her bosses, Jeanne Jackson, now the president of product and merchandising at Nike, pulled her aside after a meeting went poorly and told her, "Your ability to get to the answer fast isn't the point. You think you're the quickest person in the room. That doesn't matter. What matters is being able to bring people along with you!" Laila said, "Thank God Jeanne worked with me on that. My insecurity wasn't pretty. I remember something talent coach Marshall Goldsmith said to me in a workshop: 'You MBAs are just *dying* to add value. The next time someone's talking and you feel compelled to add value and look smart, do yourself a favor: stop, pause, and take a breath. Then ask yourself, *Will my saying this increase THEIR level of commitment?*'" Laila went on:

In interactions with others, my go-to place was to press hard and move to action. When I realized the futility of my approach—that it was off-putting—I had to figure out another strategy. I eventually realized it's not about show-ing how smart I think I am. Over time, by being open to change, I gained more perspective on my own insecurities and defense mechanisms and learned to act more compas-sionately toward others. Now, instead of just speaking up the moment something enters my mind, I know how to pause and move to a more thoughtful response. I create space by pausing, and then I react more productively.

Melanie, the general counsel at a financial services company in New York, told me about a very talented lawyer, a colleague with whom she worked at another company. "I know people who can't work with other people and just move from firm to firm," she said. "There are a couple traits I see in them: they're usually very bright; they are very passionate about what's important to them; and they usually think they know better—that their right is right." Then Melanie laughed. She said, "This one woman—super bright! She thought she knew better than the rest of us and nine times out of ten she was dead right. But her delivery was so freaking off-putting that she got *nowhere*. She'd say the sun rises in the east and we'd say it rose in the west just because she was so annoying." Melanie also said that her colleague received developmental coaching. "The CEO asked her to work with a coach. But she wasn't coacha-ble. She was so defensive, so unaware of how she came off, and she was unwilling to examine herself. She blamed her issues on our culture. She said the culture was wrong. She ended up leaving our firm. My guess is she went to the next firm for two years too, until the culture was wrong there too."

A lack of self-awareness is the single best indicator of a man-ager or executive's impending derailment. Research indicates that individuals who have an inflated sense of their skill level and understate their interpersonal issues are more than *six times likelier to derail* than those with accurate self-awareness. Of all the data I examined and research I conducted for this book, that statistic struck me the most.

In 360-degree assessments, managers who are deemed as "high potential" are closer in agreement with their raters' assessments (whether the rater is their boss, peers, or subordinates) than derailment-bound performers are with those of their raters. These high-potential managers have a more accurate understanding of themselves than average or derailed performers, and that self-awareness allows them to focus on their developmental needs and build emotional scaffolding or develop corrective measures around their personal vulnerabilities.

A Few Questions to Consider

Captain Fantastic's relational issues are fueled by a potent combination of arrogance and defensiveness, which reduces his likelihood of receiving feedback of any form. The Captain increasingly will rely on his own skewed self-perceptions and his blind spots will remain—even grow over time—and eventually one of them will derail his career. You can bet on it.

Because self-awareness is vitally important for improving interpersonal relationships, and given the extent to which many people aren't aware of their own interpersonal problems, ask yourself: *How do I respond to others under stressful conditions?* Are you calm and balanced or do you become volatile, defensive, or bossy? How would other people say you respond to them under stressful conditions? If you wonder whether you suffer from interpersonal issues, consider the following four questions:

- Do you have a propensity toward any of these six interpersonal issues: being defensive, being arrogant, showing a lack of composure, acting in a mischievous and colorful manner, being distrustful of others, or being passive?

- When you look back on past performance reviews or recent feedback, if you read carefully, perhaps even between the lines, are there any themes around interpersonal issues that you should take to heart? Look carefully, because this feedback is often delivered lightly, even in the form of a hedging comment, because the topic is sensitive. A boss might say, "You were quite forceful in that meeting and you did a decent job of getting the group to land on a decision, but let's just make sure we listen well and are sensitive to others' positions, OK?" Your ears should perk up when she moves from the singular to the plural pronoun—she's couching her feedback. What she really means is, "I'm glad we reached a decision in that meeting but you were a real pile-driver and that concerns me."

- If you sought honest, constructive criticism from peers regarding what it's like to work with you, what would you hear? If you asked your peers for three positive words and two critical words that described working with you, what would they say? Would you hear green-light words like "supportive," "collaborative," and "team-oriented" or red-light words such as "defensive," "heavy-handed," and "stubborn" (or maybe "recalcitrant" if the person was an English major)? If you can muster up the courage, ask, "Would you want me to be on an important cross functional team that you're leading?"

- If you asked the people with whom you work most closely to rate you on the following three dimensions, how would you score on a scale from one to five, from poor to great?
  - Level of *self-awareness*: How well do you understand your own personality, feelings, and behavior?

- Level of *social awareness*: How aware are you of others' feelings, needs, and concerns?
- Degree of *self-management*: Do you control your actions and take responsibility for your own behavior?

I went through this process of self-reflection around my own interpersonal issues and realized that for me it came down to two fundamental questions. First, how accurate was my mental map— did I understand how I was perceived by others, specifically the effect of my big blind spot, "mischievousness"? And, second, was I effective in communicating that I cared about the people with whom I worked and that I respected their perspectives? I figured that when I could answer "yes" to these questions, I'd be in pretty good shape from an interpersonal standpoint.

Overcoming Interpersonal Issues

Captain Fantastic is a tough case. His vessel may have to spring a leak before he's motivated to change his behavior. Therefore, to try to reach him, given the choice of a gentle prod or a two-by-four, the Captain's boss would be well advised to choose a sturdy piece of lumber. That said, if I were to counsel the Captain, or anyone else suffering from interpersonal issues, I would recommend they consider using these five corrective measures.

First, Take a 360-Degree Feedback Review

Such a review can be administered by the HR department under the watchful eye of the Captain's boss. The confidential, anonymous feedback from the people with whom he works, centering on leadership, communication, team development, peer group alignment, and interpersonal skills might well give the Captain pause.

A lack of self-awareness is what often lies behind derailment, as 90 percent of managers think they're among the top 10 percent of performers in their organizations! Those with an inflated sense of their skill level and who understate or are blind to their interpersonal issues (as demonstrated by their self-evaluation scores compared to those given them by their peers, subordinates, and bosses in 360-degree reviews) derail more often than those with accurate self-awareness. The truth of the matter, unfortunately, is that when it comes to work, most people don't have a particularly accurate self-conception and don't really know what they're good at and what they stink at. Research shows that, in general, poorer performers significantly overestimate and overstate their abilities and strong performers underestimate their own. Because of our very human propensity for inaccurate self-diagnosis it's paramount to bring in other people to help us understand our strengths, weaknesses, and vulnerabilities if we want to improve our performance. The best way to know this is through regular, ongoing performance feedback from bosses, peers, subordinates, and key outside constituents, such as customers and key partners. As much as we all groan at the prospect of going through the 360-degree feedback process, it's a tremendous way to increase our self-understanding and self-awareness.

Not surprisingly, the single biggest impediment to a useful 360-degree process is defensiveness. We can't learn if we either rationalize critical feedback or are dismissive of the entire process (which commonly happens if we feel a comment or two is inaccurate). Instead, look at whether the information contains a narrative on how we behave and where to focus our efforts. As Carl Jung said on the subject of examining and understanding one's "shadow" or "dark side" propensities: "the shadow is 90% pure gold." Much of what we have either rejected or don't want to acknowledge about our own nature can be a great asset to us if we can understand it. To know it is to manage it.

Second, Seek a Coach to Gain a Deeper Understanding of Your Blind Spots and Self-Defeating Behaviors

After going through the 360-degree feedback process, you should have an initial understanding of your areas of vulnerability. It may be the time to make an investment in a career coach, share your 360-degree feedback, and take one or two psychometric tests, which are designed to measure personality characteristics and aptitudes. They can shed additional light on areas that need attention. Two such tests, as I've mentioned, are the Hogan Personality Inventory and the Hogan Development Survey. These tests and others will enable you to delve deeper into your behaviors and motives, uncovering blind spots and areas of vulnerability you couldn't see by yourself. It will help enable you to pinpoint and more fully understand the specific personality traits that could derail your career. Although other personal assessments are available, I single out Hogan because their assessments spend quite a bit of time on "dark side" derailment propensities.

Third, Pinpoint, Examine, and Begin to Address "Overused Strengths"

We enjoy using our strengths at work, but when we go too far, our strengths become liabilities. For example, there's the manager with a very high degree of integrity who's considered by others as holier than thou and exasperating to work with; there's the team player who takes it too far and lacks independent judgment; or there's the customer-obsessed person who is unrealistic about the costs associated with implementing various customer-friendly initiatives.

A simple tool I have used to help people struggling from overusing their strengths is the "Core Quadrant Analysis." Developed by executive consultant Daniel Ofman, it can help people understand

Ofman's Core Quadrant Analysis

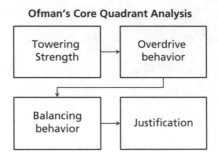

the relationship between their strengths and their weaknesses, particularly the way overused strengths become weaknesses.

There are four steps to this tool. First, identify a *towering strength*—one you rely on at work to accomplish your goals. Let's say a key strength of yours is determination. You work hard and don't stop until the job has been successfully completed. Second, sit back and consider what happens when that *strength goes into overdrive*, when you offer too much of it. Perhaps your determination turns into pushiness. In your desire to complete tasks, your determination can dissolve into brazenness or even disregard for the other person's perspective. Third, think about the *balancing behavior* you're leaving out. So with pushiness you might be missing patience or tolerance. Fourth, inquire into the balancing behavior and see if you might have an unrealized allergic reaction to it or long-held *justification* against it. When you see the quality of patience or tolerance in others, does it bother you in any way? Do you have a bias against people who demonstrate great patience or show great tolerance of others? Perhaps, deep down, you associate patient people with being lazy or slow moving. Or maybe you fear that exhibiting tolerance opens the door for others to take advantage of you. The point is, by examining the flip side of your strengths, you can uncover behavioral areas that may be holding you back.

Fourth, Just Listen

Poor listening skills hold people back in two ways. First, the failure to listen offends others and distances them from you. Two of the most fundamental human needs are being acknowledged and being understood. By not listening to others, you're denying them these needs. Second, when you fail to listen, you fail to learn. As the fourteenth Dalai Lama said, "When you talk, you are only repeating what you already know. But if you listen, you may learn something new." So never miss a good chance to shut up, watch, listen, and learn.

Here are six simple listening tips:

- Adopt an attitude that everyone can teach you *something*. In every conversation, consider that the person with whom you're talking knows something that you don't.
- Listen without interrupting, avoiding the tendency to jump in and "add value" to their point. (I often have to curb this tendency.)
- Actively listen—nod and jot down notes, etc.
- When the other person is finished, ask clarifying questions.
- Paraphrase what the other person said to signal that you listened and understand her point.
- Don't instantly judge her point—that can come later. Good listeners don't automatically offer advice or a solution or a counterpoint to what they've heard. They first determine what the other person is seeking from the conversation.

Fifth, Work to Maintain Your Equanimity

Equanimity is a feeling of calm self-possession—regardless of circumstances. Self-defeating behaviors are most likely to pop out in charged situations, often when you lose your bearing in the heat of the moment. As a counter to stressful situations, I have a mantra I recite to myself: *Be the participant and the observer.* I try to distance myself from my internal swirl by imagining that I'm transported out of my skin, watching myself perform from a safe distance, offering the occasional helpful suggestion to Carter. I like the metaphor of watching myself move on the dance floor but from the safety of the balcony. Away from the fray, my perspective is clearer. From up above, I can see how the various dancers are dancing, who's leading the band, and what song they're playing. I can gain a clearer view on the reality of the situation. My goal in using these mental devices is to create a little space—a little pause in order to reflect—between the situation as it's occurring and my reaction to it. This small degree of detachment makes it easier for me to observe how others are reacting to me. Are they smiling and nodding? Are they leaning forward, a look of concentration on their face? Or is their body language closed, leaning back, arms crossed? Are they staring into my eyes or are they focused on some imaginary point on my forehead, eyes glazed over?

*

As we progress in our careers, work problems become more complex and interpersonal dynamics more nuanced. More challenging work creates internal pressure, which often activates our interpersonal vulnerabilities. If unaware, we often respond by being increasingly defensive, or abrasive, or passive. Talented people may be able to get by with a glaring interpersonal issue at a lower level, when they're primarily evaluated on completing independent tasks, but not at higher levels, where their success in larger cross functional assignments will come from the broad-based support of others. As Korn Ferry leadership researcher Guangrong Dai said, "Some personality traits will benefit people early in their career [but] hurt them later. Managers must become aware of how their strengths can eventually hurt them through overuse."

Therefore, we need to uncover, examine, and address our developmental opportunities early on when the stakes aren't as high. Later on in our career, when our time is highly desired and our work calendar is packed with meetings and trips, we will find it harder to find the necessary time to retrench, seek counsel, and effectively address a wayward personality trait.

It certainly is possible to address and remedy the harmful behaviors that impede our ability to work well with others. Take the case of a Captain Fantastic named Robert, whose career as a management consultant took off in his thirties due to his ability to bring in new clients for his firm. Robert was smart, engaging, and bold—when he pitched prospective customers, they believed in his ability to improve their business performance. As a result of his skills as a rainmaker, Robert became the youngest managing director of his large management consulting firm and was put in charge of a large region of the western part of the United States. That's when he ran into trouble. As a managing director, he was required to spend a significant amount of time on administrative matters, such as budget management, capital resource allocation, and employee training and development. He had to work with "all these corporate types on the overall strategy of the company and do all this coordination work." He didn't know how to do it—he had little training in matters of business administration. To make matters worse, given his bold, brash, confident manner, his pride made him incapable of asking others for help. He was used to others coming *to him* for help! Because of his lack of knowledge in these administrative matters, he became insecure, which, given his personality traits, manifested in him becoming a blowhard. In a meeting that examined the pros and cons of two prospective performance management software systems, Robert came to the meeting late, listened for five minutes, and then barked, "Oh, come on! We're overcomplicating this! Let's just pick a solution and implement it. Either way, it's not going to be perfect for God's sake!" In addition to "we're overcomplicating this!" a second favorite expression of Robert's that further alienated people in the support functions of his firm was, "In every company, there are revenue centers and cost centers. You want to be in the former." Over a period of one year, Robert alienated enough "cost center" people that they began to avoid working with him. As a result, his region's business-planning efforts were uncoordinated and sloppy and after one year, due to his poor leadership, his firm stripped away his regional responsibilities—the important resource allocation aspects of his job, such as creating a strategic plan for the area and coordinating the selling efforts of the firm's consultants across the region—essentially making him more or less an individual contributor.

Because Robert was a challenge to deal with, no one in the firm coached or counseled him. He received little feedback before his responsibilities were taken away. No one made him aware of the damaging effect of his bold, insensitive interpersonal style and tried to help him improve. So the organization was complicit in his derailment—none of the senior partners or the head of HR told Robert he was doing a poor job, and not only because they feared his response but because they enjoyed the revenue he generated from his client selling skills and didn't want to risk him leaving the firm. So they took a soft stance, saying they wanted to "free him up to get back to what he was incredibly talented in doing."

But Robert was a smart fellow and was able to interpret the subtext of what happened. Even though his title hadn't changed, his responsibilities were taken away and he understood that he'd experienced what he called "a soft demotion." So Robert asked his firm to spring for an executive coach. And they did, because they loved his ability to generate revenue. Robert's coach immediately conducted a 360-degree feedback on him, interviewing subordinates, peers, and senior-most managers of the firm. Robert was stunned by the feedback—absolutely shell shocked. He had never received real feedback in his entire career at the firm. He said he didn't want to be the guy described in the feedback: "Robert can be a bully"; "He's strong coffee—bold and loud and overly sure of himself"; "He doesn't respect the support groups that enable him to succeed"; "Robert has the poorest listening skills of any of our senior leaders—he loves to hear himself talk and is dismissive of others' perspectives."

Robert said that once he licked his wounds for a few days and "realized that rationalizing away the feedback would keep me in the same position I'm in now," he worked with his coach to improve in three areas. First, he began to develop an understanding of the triggers that usually set him off—which often had to do with "excessive process and internal red tape—mind-numbing meetings and cover-your-ass paperwork that kept me from working with clients." He then worked on his self-restraint, trying to do a better job of not reacting in a destructive way when triggered.

Second, Robert learned to listen better. He began to develop the discipline of not weighing in with his point of view until he'd solicited the opinion of others around the table and magically, he said, "I began to understand why others were requesting certain things that I previously thought were idiotic."

And, third, Robert began asking for help. He came to realize that asking others for their assistance wasn't a show of weakness and resulted in him being viewed as more accessible to others.

As Robert's performance began to improve, it didn't go unnoticed. The senior partners and head of HR saw and heard of the changes in Robert's managerial style, and, eighteen months later, when the firm decided to open a new office in the Pacific Northwest to serve their burgeoning technology practice, Robert was asked to oversee the region, which he gratefully accepted. Now, five years later, Robert said, "Things are going well. While I still don't love the management aspects of my job as much as working directly with clients, it isn't a liability like it was. Plus, I know enough to hire good managers around me—people who are better at business planning and administration—so I can spend more of my time at what I'm good at—building strong client relationships."

Will Captain Fantastic, presented at the beginning of the chapter, end up derailing? If he does, will he have the same success as Robert in getting back on track? I've encountered many Captain Fantastics in my career—and I'm sure you have, too. I would bet that the Captain's job will be secure as long as he's able to post good numbers, as companies often turn a blind eye to bad behavior when business results are positive. But eventually the Captain will be unable to muscle his way to beating his operating plan, and when that happens, he'll find himself alone on an island, with no allies caring to rescue him. When that day comes, the Captain will either get fired or, if he's an extraordinarily talented asset for the company, be assigned an executive coach who will attempt to rehabilitate him. That will be his ultimate IQ test—will he have the courage to look inside himself and recognize and address his destructive personality traits, or will he avoid painful self-reflection and assign blame elsewhere? Will the Captain answer the call to action and go through the Hero Journey, entering the dark forest, encountering personal demons, and ultimately slaying dragons to emerge back into the light, or will he shirk under the weight of the task? That is the question.

CHAPTER 2

THE SOLO FLIER

"Step Aside, I've Got This."

S arah the Solo Flier has been on a roll ever since grade school. All of her life, a standard of performance was set before her and she surpassed it. Whether it's winning the coveted Golden Apple at the competitive Fairfield Middle School Science Fair, writing her honors thesis on US–Soviet arms control and disarmament at Kenyon College, or performing a supply chain efficiency analysis that reduced her company's shipping carrier cost by 10 percent, like the postman, she delivers, rain or shine. Her heroes are the irrepressible Eleanor Roosevelt and Facebook's chief operating officer Sheryl Sandberg and her favorite time of day is *now*. Friendly, forthright, and unswervingly efficient, she is an asset to any company lucky enough to have her as an employee.

And then, given her strong performance as an individual contributor, the Solo Flier was promoted into her first substantial managerial job, as manager of sourcing and supply chain operations.

In this position, she oversees a team of seven purchasing agents and is responsible for managing the product sourcing and order flow through the distribution chain of a $750 million midwestern consumer package company selling an array of personal hygiene products to consumers through national retailers.

Three months later, sitting in a Starbucks across the street from her office at 3:00 p.m. on a Monday, Sarah holds an untouched cup of coffee and notices a slight ripple across the surface of the liquid. She is shaking—the result of a large dose of adrenaline released from her adrenal glands after taking a shelling in her weekly staff meeting. It was an insurrection, really, and after the meeting she'd escaped to Starbucks to collect herself.

She did not understand it—not one bit. She thought she was doing a good job in her managerial position. Sure, she was managing her new team closely, but so did Steve Jobs when he returned to Apple to clean things up! And she set a fine example for others to follow. She got her hands dirty and worked her tail off. No task was too small for her to take on. Why, once she'd gone into the company's central warehouse, during the heat of summer, to conduct a physical inventory in order to get an accurate count of a new product that was starting to take off! Exacting but fair, she had given the people who worked for her explicit directions to improve the sourcing process, such as telling them how to build complex pivot tables in their spreadsheets to properly analyze raw material costs. The performance of her department was improving—so how on earth did she find herself in this mess?!

Sarah replayed the painful sequence of events from her staff meeting. As always, she had told her team members to fill out their weekly report of completed activities (RCAs) before the meeting and to come prepared to share progress with the team. When it came time for Fred, an old-school product sourcing specialist who had been plugging away at the company for twenty years, to share, he'd said, "Sorry, but I didn't have time to fill it out this time." When she had pressed, he mumbled something inaudible. When she said, "Excuse me?" he said, "Look, I'm a bit busy doin' my job to account for every bathroom break I take." Others in the room had snickered. Then she told Fred they'd take the conversation offline, and Fred said, "Actually, why don't we keep it online? You may want to hear from others on fillin' out these so-called RCAs." And then the levee had broken, and she was awash with complaints from everyone in the room. She heard the words "bureaucratic," "micromanager," and "overcontrolling." Fred had created a new word that the group seemed to take to: "report-o-mania."

Although she thought she'd done a good job handling the situation—she listened to their complaints without becoming too defensive or losing her cool—when the meeting concluded she needed to regroup and evaluate what had happened. Now, sitting at Starbucks, she was not only apprehensive but truly stumped. Her clear, straightforward style had always worked before. Why not now? Was it her, or the sometimes slow-moving people she managed? Yes, in terms of years on the job, they were more experienced than she was. Yes, she had a high standard of performance and didn't mince words. But she'd been given the promotion for a reason—because she got results! Was there some middle ground she needed to explore? Did she need to pull back a bit from her hands-on management style? Did she need to downshift and become less exacting and directive? And what would happen if she shifted into a lower gear—would she maintain her effectiveness? Or would she lose her edge and be less successful? Regardless, it appeared that for the first time in her life, her "up and to the right" career trajectory seemed in danger of veering off course. What was her next move? She wasn't sure.

Solo Fliers fail to build high-performing teams due to:

- Overmanaging;
- Hiring poorly, often assembling a team in their own image instead of a team with diverse skills and perspectives;
- Not communicating well, in particular not explaining business priorities or the strategic context for decisions;
- Avoiding conflict or not resolving it promptly;
- Not motivating or developing subordinates, resulting in low morale and high turnover; and
- Not driving alignment between their team and other departments in order to garner the necessary resources to successfully accomplish projects that have cross group dependencies.

Questions for the Solo Flier

The first thing Sarah the Solo Flier has to understand is that the very attributes that got her the promotion won't allow her to succeed in her new position. Although her hands-on approach catapulted her into a managerial position at a young age, it simply won't work with a group of seasoned sourcing agents. What her new team needed was someone to set a clear direction with tangible performance goals and then help them by securing organizational support and resources to accomplish them. The team needed a team leader, not a team overseer.

The Solo Flier's case is not uncommon. When many of us get into a significant managerial position, our first inclination is to hold on tight, control as much as humanly possible, and try to micromanage our way to a successful outcome. But the outcome turns into a double whammy: we're exhausted and the people who work for us are annoyed or, worse yet, demotivated. The Solo Flier had the wherewithal to pull back and consider what had happened in her team meeting that ran amok. She needs to continue to go down that path of self-reflection and make corrective changes before she experiences a career derailment event.

If, like the Solo Flier, you think you may have team management issues, here are some questions to consider and also to ask people who report to you and peers who've watched you manage others:

- Are you impatient with people when they get stuck and don't know the answer? Do you tend to swoop in and do the work yourself for the sake of expediency?
- If you asked each of your team members to recount their top three individual goals for the quarter (or the year) and the corresponding success metrics, could they do so quickly and easily? Or would they say something like, "Well, it really depends on what's important to you, as my boss."
- Would you hear a consistent response if you asked each of your team members, independently, the three most important team goals for the quarter (or the year)?
- If you asked each team member whether internal team issues were resolved quickly or slowly, what would they say?
- If you asked your direct reports whether you spent enough time with them on their professional development, what would they say?
- What percentage of time are you talking versus listening in your staff meetings?
- When was the last time you asked one of your direct reports about his life outside of the job?

Where They Go Wrong

Janice, a talented senior-level merchandising executive who worked for a Fortune 500 retailer, is a strong team manager who has worked with a number of Solo Fliers and has helped to improve their performance. One woman with whom she worked especially piqued her interest:

> I wanted to hire this super talented merchant. I did reference checks on her and people would sigh and say, "She'll build an incredible business for you, but it will come at a price. She has a burning ambition and has blinders on. She'll try to do it all herself and there'll be plenty of collateral damage." But she was so talented that I brought her on board anyway. I put her on a small team and she did well. But when I put her on a bigger assignment, and she had to manage a larger team, she ran into trouble. She wasn't methodical about how she managed her team. She didn't set expectations— goals and objectives and KPIs (key performance indicators). She didn't follow sound managerial practices—having staff meetings, touching base with people on a one-to-one basis, etc. She ran her business based on her own gut instincts. Her results in our corporate opinion survey that gauges employee engagement were terrible. In particular, her team was not clear on the direction they were headed. They didn't understand how their work fit within the group and the company's direction.

But, Janice continued, "To her great credit, after we went over her team's engagement results, she put her head down and really worked on it. The issues were clear and well quantified so we put a very specific plan together and then tracked the changes in the engagement scores on an ongoing basis. A year later her employee engagement scores were up twenty points—a massive amount. She's since left the company and now she's a senior vice president at another huge retailer."

Janice went on to say something reminiscent of Sarah the Solo Flier's issue:

It's really hard to make that shift from being an amazing individual contributor to being an effective manager—learning how to explain the big picture, inspiring a team and overseeing execution without becoming an impediment. When people get into managerial positions, it's common to manage too closely—hang on too tight or want to do it themselves— and that doesn't go over well. So they overcompensate and step away too quickly. That doesn't work either. Or they give too much feedback, then not enough feedback. You have to be tuned in to your team and seek feedback in order to find the right balance.

People like the Solo Flier who suffer from team management issues often create problems for themselves in three ways: overmanaging, not building an effective team, and not leading the team.

Overmanaging

Finding the balance between over- and undermanaging a team can be challenging, but overmanaging is the more common reason why people run into trouble. It's common for overmanagers to meddle, swoop in ("here, let me show you how to format that presentation"), and fail to empower team members to have discretion over their work. It's no surprise, then, that people on the team find their efforts thwarted and often lose their sense of autonomy and desire to take the initiative.

These managers, like the Solo Flier, are usually poor delegators. Because they were strong individual contributors, they tend to revert to that behavior and try to do the work themselves. "In build-ing and leading teams," observes Candice Frankovelgia, a coach at the Center for Creative Leadership, "we run into these fabulous performers who get a team and still behave like all the ideas have to come from them. This creates bottlenecks and dampens innova-tion." This goes back to my earlier point about overused strengths becoming liabilities. The very same assertiveness and initiative that helps put managers like Sarah the Solo Flier on the fast track can become detrimental when they transition from being individ-ual contributors to team managers. New managers must not only learn to work with and through others instead of being self-reliant, they also need to move from a narrow task orientation to a broader strategic orientation, which requires the ability to be effective in the context of the broader organization, with all its internal and external constituents.

Ruth Malloy, a consultant for executive search firm Spen-cer Stuart's Leadership Advisory Services, said, "If you're a high achiever, you get promoted and tend to still want to do your pre-vious job. The problem is, as you ascend, your role broadens. You can't be good at everything. You need to rely on others." For many talented managers, skilled in and rewarded for "doing," the shift to manager is a hard one. The issue of overmanaging isn't confined to freshly minted managers either. Middle and senior-level manag-ers often swoop in and meddle, whether it's because they're trying to, in their mind, "help expedite the process" or simply because they feel comfortable being in the middle of the work. Eric Lau-terbach, the president of the consumer division at Peet's Coffee & Tea, told me, "Often in my career, I've seen seasoned managers fail in their jobs because they don't play at the right level. They try to do the job that's one level below them, because that's comfort-able for them. They know how to do it. Then it cascades down: the next level of managers do the job one level below them and things become dysfunctional. People are confused about roles and responsibilities; they get discouraged, and eventually don't want to work in that senior manager's group."

Not Building an Effective Team

The propensity to overmanage and swoop down to do the work yourself can also stem from hiring poorly and not taking steps to build a diverse and talented team with complementary skills. In particular, I've seen hiring managers run into trouble by not being rigorous in the interviewing process. Amid their flurry of activity, they don't take the time to create a thoughtful and comprehensive candidate job description that describes the role, its responsibilities, and its skill requirements/job qualifications and that weighs the relative importance of the position's key activities.

A thorough job description is essential; it is a guide that allows those conducting the interviews to probe the candidate in the most important areas. Also, managers must take the time to prepare each interviewer with a list of questions or areas to probe, in order to get a full view of the candidate's capabilities (and also ensure the candidate isn't repeatedly asked the same questions).

In addition, managers who struggle building their team usually take too long to hire in areas where they have gaps. They don't make recruiting a top priority and drag their feet before they make the hard decision to move an ineffective team member out of the group. This problem isn't limited to first-time managers. Even experienced C-suite executives get caught in this trap, as reported in a 2015 McKinsey study examining how effective executives were in transitioning into new positions. A surprising number—72 percent of the 1,195 executives surveyed—said they wished they'd moved faster to get the right people on their team and move the wrong people off. And when asked to identify which activities were most important to the success of their transition, 86 percent cited mobilizing their team to function as a high-performing group by establishing clear priorities and performance metrics and allocating the workload.

Not Leading the Team

This issue often is exhibited in four ways. The first is doing a poor job of communicating business priorities and not providing the necessary strategic context for tasks or assignments. Team members, then, don't understand why they're doing what they're doing and how their work fits within the overall strategy of the team, the department, or the organization. Not knowing the end goal or purpose behind an assignment is not only demotivating; it also fails to leverage the capabilities of the workers and doesn't give them the freedom to consider other ways to solve the problem or complete the task. If they knew the end goal, they may have a better solution than the boss. For example, when I was at Walmart.com and was given responsibility for managing the merchandise function in addition to marketing, I was dissatisfied with our Monday-morning merchandise meetings. They felt rote and very "rearview mirror"–oriented to me, consisting of the category merchants reporting on their sales and margin rates and their inventory levels from the prior week. I wasn't sure how to change it, so I posed the question to my direct reports: How can I make this Monday merchandise meeting more about building the business and not merely a boring reporting of the numbers? Within five minutes a great idea emerged from the team: have every category merchandise manager lead off their portion of the meeting by bringing in and showing something that struck them from their weekend market tours. They would share something that caught their attention and pointed to a marketplace trend—a new product, a technology device, a new service, a new retailer, an interesting and timely article in a magazine or newspaper, a powerful advertisement—and explain how the item represented might be applied to build our business. I loved the idea and immediately applied it to the merchandise meeting. The merchants enjoyed this stimulating session because it stoked their creativity. They observed, captured, and then applied what they saw into something the company could do better or differently: "If you saw *x*, what's the application? If *yes*, then *what*?"

A second team leadership issue concerns managers who let team-related issues fester, reducing group effectiveness and dragging down morale. These managers have trouble resolving interpersonal, resource-allocation, or work flow/process–related problems in a timely way. Early in my career, I had a boss who had been dubbed "The Artful Dodger" by my peers and me. When we approached him to seek resolution over a point of contention—for example, who was responsible for a murky area within our retail selling efforts, or who owned a budget spending area—he had trouble umpiring and calling "balls and strikes" and thereby alleviating the point of friction. He'd hem and haw and suggest some sort of joint ownership approach that satisfied no one. We'd often leave his office more confused than when we entered.

A third team leadership issue is failing to develop the functional and managerial skills of direct reports. Jackie, an editorial director of a book publishing firm in New York, fell into this trap but was able to dig her way out. Jackie received a big promotion and began managing design and production in addition to her editorial responsibilities. But with her forceful, hands-on management style, she had trouble managing a larger, more diverse team where a more nuanced managerial approach was required. "I'm a strong personality," Jackie said. She continued:

> If I'm not careful, I can create anxiety in people. I've been told that when I enter the room, the atmosphere can change, sometimes in a good way, but sometimes not so good. People

might sit up a little straighter. They may not be as relaxed as before. When I was promoted into a bigger job, I realized, by the reaction that I was receiving, that I was coming on too strong with my new team, who needed some TLC. The production department already felt like "the editorial depart-ment swallowed us" and then I—someone from editorial—get promoted and come storming in. But through coaching and a lot of self-examination, I've learned to pull back, listen really carefully to what my team members are saying and just be patient. Patience is the key. I need to let them discover the solutions themselves and if they're struggling I can just move them along the path here and there, but carefully. I've realized that it's my job to create the right environment for them to discover the answer themselves, not to show them the way to do things. I still catch myself sometimes. I'll hear myself say, "No—that's not the right way!" instead of being patient and saying, "OK, take me through your approach." But because I'm aware of my tendency to dive in, I do it much less than I used to.

Fourth, managing the team's context can be challenging and a problem for even experienced leaders. Managing team members one-on-one isn't the same as managing the team, as Linda Hill, a professor at Harvard Business School, has written: "[Managers] conceive of their people-management role as building the most effective relationships they can with each individual subordinate and erroneously equate managing the team with managing the indi-viduals." Being effective in managing your team's context includes:

- Aligning key constituents behind your team's business objectives and lobbying the various powers-that-be to secure needed resources for your team;

- Building bridges and developing strong relations with other departments and collaborators with whom you're dependent, ensuring they're aligned with you on key initiatives; and
- Monitoring the competitive environment on an ongoing basis and making adjustments to business strategy based on competitive and marketplace assessments.

One of my own mistakes taught me the importance of gaining cross functional alignment between my team and other departments. When I was a product marketing manager at Frito-Lay in the early 1990s, I was part of a team that developed a new, delicious black bean dip. It was an all-natural thing of beauty made up of black beans, onions, garlic, jalapeños, and that was about it. No nasty fillers or additives. It was manufactured through a "retortion" pasteurization method (where we heated the product by flushing it with hot water while its jars rotated in large, oven-like vats) that did not necessitate adding vinegar to the product to kill microorganisms. Without the vinegar, which nearly every other competitive product contained, the black bean dip had a smooth taste that scored through the roof in our consumer panel taste tests.

I launched the product and watched it fail, not because of poor quality but due to lack of communication and alignment between the marketing and field sales groups. Frito-Lay's sales force was so excited about this new dip that they jacked up their initial order quantities and expanded its selling footprint to geographies outside of the ones I'd identified as a good fit for the product. They slammed it into full national distribution rather than tactically ordering it for certain geographies that fit the right geodemographic consumer profile, the western and southwestern United States, in particular. As a result, the product didn't turn fast enough on retail shelves and was especially slow moving in supermarkets across the eastern and northern parts of the country. Although the product supply department warned me about our sales force overordering, I was unable to convince the regional sales vice presidents in the east and north to cut back on their order quantities. Why? I hadn't developed strong enough relationships with them to convince them that this was a niche product that would do well in certain parts of the country and not in others. At the time I blamed the sales force for the product's failure. Later on I realized that if I had taken the time to get out into the field and tour with the sales managers and vice presidents, I would have been able to get them on the phone prior to launch and convince them to cut back on their order quantities and do a tactical, regional rollout. It was a mistake I did not repeat. Throughout the rest of my career at Frito-Lay, I blocked the time out of my schedule to get out of headquarters and into the field and tour with sales managers every other week.

Getting Better at Building and Leading Teams

How do people like the Solo Flier become more effective team managers and leaders? If I were counseling her or someone else struggling to build and lead a team, I would have them examine five areas that could help develop a more effective managerial and leadership style.

Demonstrate That You Care

Speak less, listen more, and show that you care about your team members. First, take the time to get to know them, asking questions and expressing interest in both their work and their nonwork lives. Listen carefully. Seek to understand before being understood. By doing so, your team members will reward you in many ways. They will work harder, become advocates of your agenda,

and, importantly, cut you some slack—looking past your own foi-
bles and errors. I've often heard managers say, "I believe in keeping work and personal lives separate. At work, I don't engage with
others on personal terms." And I would respond, "What are we—
robots? Work is made up of people. When work is performed at its
best, it's *because* it's personal! It matters because of the esprit de
corps of a group of people who care about each other and work
together to achieve a goal." And if I was revved up, I'd go on to
say, "Soldiers aren't loyal to an abstraction—the United States of
America—they're loyal to their squad and their sergeant. Workers
aren't loyal to their company so much as they're loyal to their peers
and their team leader." So don't leave your personality at the door.
Engage with your team members at a personal, not just "professional," level. As Maya Angelou said, "I've learned that people will
forget what you said, people will forget what you did, but people
will never forget how you made them feel."

Second, take the time to understand the career goals and
aspirations of your team members and help them make progress
toward them. Investing in their professional skill development is
an important way of demonstrating that you care. Work with them
to appraise their current skill level and gaps; devise a developmental plan with them; then meet on a regular basis (perhaps quarterly) to discuss progress. Research shows that at least 70 percent of
a worker's skill development comes from having challenging tasks
and assignments, and the best way to develop people is through
"on-the-job" training, which you can do by offering stretch assignments and tasks that will force them out of their comfort zone and
allow them to further develop their skills.

Third, be cognizant of the cultural norms of your team (their
collective set of beliefs and attitudes—basically, "how we do things
around here"), so you won't step on land mines and will know the
best way to motivate them as a team. There's a good chance that

Sarah the Solo Flier, with her intense focus on efficiency, had yet to take the time to get to know each of her team members—their personalities, aspirations, and goals—in order to begin to gain their trust and loyalty and manage them well. It's also likely that she didn't take the time to understand the cultural norms of the team so she could understand how to manage the group effectively. For example, if she knew that her new team, made up of veteran product supply sourcing agents, greatly valued their autonomy and prided themselves on the collective experience level of the team ("Jim's the baby in the group and he has nine years of sourcing experience!"), surely she would have managed them differently. I imagine she would have thought twice before forcing them to do rote paperwork—in this case the RCA. Instead, she may have kicked off her first team meeting by saying, "With your amazing 125 years of collective experience in sourcing, I doubt I'm going to teach you anything new about the process of sourcing. But by understanding your needs, I may be able to help us secure more resources to allow you to do your jobs even better."

I feel for the Solo Flier. It's hard to take over a new (and in this case experienced) team. The first instinct is to show that you know your stuff and to exert control. But that's not the right move to make. The first step is to ask questions and listen carefully to the answers in order to understand the situation in which you find yourself.

Set a Clear Course

I've seen many teams become ineffective and flounder because people are demotivated by a lack of group direction as well as a lack of clarity on how their work fits into the overall strategy. Make sure you can answer the following fundamental questions from your team:

- *As a team, what is our end goal?* Work with your team members to establish a clear direction. Don't hand them a strategy on a silver platter—enlist them in the creation of the game plan. That will create buy-in and commitment to the end goal.

- *How will we know when we've reached it?* You achieve what you measure by having clear KPIs for both the team and each team member so everyone can measure and track progress against the end goal. (When I conduct my one-to-one meetings with people reporting to me, I usually cover three areas for approximately twenty minutes each: a quick business performance update against their KPIs; a discussion of their progress against key initiatives; and their people and resource needs.)

- *How does each person's job fit in to the overall strategy?* Ensure your individual team members know how their work fits into the overall strategy of the group and furthers progress toward key goals. This is an essential aspect of job motivation. In conjunction, help your team members understand how their work relates to the work of others on the team. How do the different roles fit together, and where are the delineations and handoffs? You want to avoid role confusion whenever possible. Stay on top of these areas *constantly*. Hold team meetings where members provide key project updates and the team can discuss work flow and handoffs and make decisions around areas of overlap or joint accountability. As Harvard's Linda Hill said, "Clarity seldom happens or holds for long by itself. Group relationships and roles, especially in organizations passing through rapid change, tend to move toward confusion."

To set a clear course, you have to confront team-related problems directly. You can't assume they'll go away on their own. If you don't address festering issues, whether it's a personality conflict between team members or a resource allocation issue, you will lose credibility and your team's performance will suffer. Being conflict averse by nature, I have had to work mightily to improve in this area. "Conflict averse" used to come up just about every year in my performance review during my twenties and thirties. In particular, I was guilty of not asserting myself enough in charged situations with my peers, usually over disagreements about resource allocation and strategic decisions around which initiatives to pursue and which to kill. Sometimes my lack of assertiveness hurt my team, who sometimes didn't receive the support they needed from me to do their jobs. This weakness came to a head when I was in my late thirties and a vice president of marketing at Walmart.com. I was sufficiently embarrassed by my behavior that I vowed to remedy the tendency. It was during a big meeting where Walmart's corporate brass flew in from Bentonville, Arkansas, to our Walmart.com office in the Bay Area to propose a direction around how to increase our market share in the nascent but quickly growing digital music category. My team at Walmart.com didn't agree with the strategy proposed by the Walmart executives, which involved, in part, developing our own music device to compete against Apple's iPod.

I agreed with my team that the hardware manufacturing business was not a competency of Walmart's and we would waste resources by pursuing this strategy. But I hemmed and hawed and wasn't forceful and convincing in stating my perspective to the Walmart executives. An influential Walmart executive from Bentonville dismissed my point of view, saying, "We need to do *something* to preserve our market share in the music business and this [creating a hardware device to compete against the iPod] is what we should do." At that point, there was an awkward silence. Then one of the people who worked in my group swooped in and communicated forcefully to the Walmart executives why their proposed strategy was not the right course of action and that the Walmart. com team categorically disagreed with it. He closed by saying, "We have much bigger fish to fry than this. If we do what you propose, we'd have to pull resources off several Internet-based projects that have a much higher return on investment than this—and a couple are projects that make it faster and easier for customers to shop inside Walmart stores." He went on to briefly explain one of our big Walmart store-enhancing initiatives that would not be complete if we were to pursue the proposed direction on digital music. When he finished, the most senior Walmart executive in the room stared at him. My team member returned the stare. Then the top dog responded with, "OK—then we won't do it. These other projects your team is working on sound more important."

When the meeting adjourned and the Walmart officers left our office, my boss, John Fleming, the CEO of Walmart.com, who had attended the meeting as a fly on the wall, said, "Carter, in my office, *now*." He proceeded to dress me down, talking about the lack of backbone I demonstrated in needing one of my team members to do my bidding for me. I was completely embarrassed. I left John's office, found the manager, and apologized to him for not doing my job and also complimented him for his guts and eloquence. I then went into my office and stewed.

I realized I could no longer put off working on this weakness; I needed to change and find a way to be more effective in setting a clear course by communicating my position in times of conflict. I read good books like *Crucial Conversations* and *The Power of a Positive No*. I participated in conflict management role-play simulations. I sought continued counsel from my boss, John, an ex-hockey player who had absolutely no problem with confrontation. (I think at times he got a kick out of it.) And over time I did improve quite a bit in this area and was eventually promoted into John's job, where I was forced to deal with conflict on a daily basis.

One final point on setting a clear course. As a leader, it's important to your team that you explain your decisions. When you make meaningful decisions, seek the counsel of your team, or at least share your thought process and how you arrived at your decision. What was the issue? What were the factors you examined? How did you weight them? How did you reach your conclusion? Bring them along with you—it will not only motivate your team to be included, but it's also an important part of their learning process. (Follow the three "E's" of fair process decision making— *Engagement*: involve them in the decision; *Explanation*: help them understand the reason for the final decision; and *Expectations*: let them know the ramifications of the decision, how it will affect them, and the new rules of the game.)

In your staff meetings, reserve a little time to inform them on enterprise-level happenings. Explain to them why your company made a big acquisition, sold off a division, or killed a product line. Debate it for a few minutes. I am a big believer in managerial transparency. Withholding information and managing opaquely is a poor way to lead your team. The people working for you are smart. They can help you solve problems. If you aren't forthcoming, your team members will smell a rat and know you're hiding something. That will then create unnecessary organizational swirl. It will also demotivate them. The people on your team are, more likely than not, hard workers who deserve to know what's going on in the place they're spending well over two-thirds of their waking hours.

Be Patient and Strive to Maintain Your Objectivity

One of the most challenging aspects of leading a team is remaining open-minded and objective. Most good decisions come from seeking a constant stream of feedback. We all have to work on the lost art of listening to find the gem in the feedback. As managers, we all enter into situations with our predispositions and natural biases and it's hard to set them aside and listen objectively. (The Solo Flier found this out when she wasn't tuned in to her team's dissatisfied rumblings, which then turned into an insurrection.) Good listening involves patience and careful attention. We have to become open and observant and listen for the subtext, the buried gem, the quiet sounds. As the thirteenth-century Persian poet Rumi said, "Every tree and plant in the meadow seemed to be dancing, those which average eyes would see as fixed and still." When we're able to be quiet, patient, and open to what others are saying, the best course of action often reveals itself. To do this, we have to be cognizant of our biases, about both the messenger and the message. There is well-documented research that shows managers' biases in the way they behave toward people who they perceive to be "strong performers" versus "weak performers." There is a "set up to fail" syndrome, where bosses show little interest in "weaker" subordinates' comments or suggestions and rarely ask them for input about organizational matters.

To reduce your natural biases and remain objective use these rules of thumb:

- Don't lead with your answer; instead, ask open-ended questions that don't tip your hand on your perspective but instead allow your team members to explore the possibilities. For example, instead of saying, "Do you like the blue-steel logo as much as I do?" you might say, "Which of these logo designs do you think better communicates our value proposition to twenty-five- to thirty-nine-year-old single men—and why?"
- Ask follow-up questions. Often, subordinates' first answers may be tentative. When you show interest by asking follow-up questions, they will sense your true interest in their perspective and will open up and tell you more.

- Play back and synthesize what your team members have said, so they know they've been heard.

Maintaining your objectivity also requires the ability to "understand your default mode of communication," says executive coach Brooke Vuckovic, which for many leaders occurs by being directive or trying to problem solve for team members. "But that's not necessarily what the person at the receiving end needs. For example, there are times a direct report comes to a leader looking to pressure test or validate an idea but does not want explicit direction. Subordinates can feel unappreciated or even irritated if their boss, instead of seeking to understand what's required of them, moves to a default mode of telling the subordinate what to do."

There are simple tools that allow you to tune in to what's most important to the other person during an interaction and therefore how you should approach it. Vuckovic cites the "VIVID" model as a simple and useful framework.

- Does your subordinate just need to *vent*? He might be saying, in essence, "I don't need your direction. I just need to vent, but I will figure this out."
- Or is he coming to you because he needs more *information*? He may be seeking clarification on a point of yours or access to an additional piece of data.
- Or your subordinate may be looking for *validation*. He may just need a dose of assurance or your blessing on the way he is approaching a problem.
- Or he may be looking to riff with you on the *idea*—to brainstorm and kick around various ideas.
- Last, he may indeed be seeking your *direction*, wanting to explicitly know what you want him to do. Be careful, though: bosses often assume their team members are

looking for direction when instead they are looking for one of the above four areas in their interaction with you.

Delegate to Motivate

It's sobering to realize that, as a manager, you're no longer the master of your own destiny. The higher you rise in an organization, the less work you do yourself; you rely on others to do it for you. So it's critical to learn to let go. It's a lot easier to do that if you've set a clear direction and developed goals and objectives for your team members with measurable success metrics. This will allow you to "trust but verify," as Ronald Reagan was known to say. If the people on your team understand what's expected of them, it's much easier for you to delegate. And delegating tasks and projects will free up your time to focus on leading the team, not just managing it. If you're not clear on what to and what not to delegate, discuss these three questions with your team members: (1) "Where could you use more help from me?"; (2) "Where could you use less help from me?"; and (3) "In what areas could I step away completely and let you manage without me?"

By deliberately and carefully loosening your hold on the reins, you'll create a climate where people will want to do their best. They'll be motivated by your trust and their ownership. When Sarah the Solo Flier was promoted into her new position, she would have been well served to ask her experienced team members the above three questions to gauge where she could add the most value. Stuart Kaplan, the director of leadership recruiting at Google, calls this move from manager to motivator "the growth into a new identity." He said, "As you rise in an organization, you realize you need to approach things differently. You realize you cannot do it yourself. You can't do it by being hands-on and directing traffic. You realize you must release your old ways—the very ways that made you very successful! The good leaders get there—they do the necessary soul-searching and come to the conclusion that their role is to set direction, then delegate and motivate."

Top job motivators include job challenge, accomplishing something worthwhile, learning new things, working with people you like, and having autonomy. (Compensation, although obviously important, is never at the top of the list.) Daniel Pink, in his best seller *Drive*, discusses three important motivators: autonomy, mastery, and purpose. So enrich your subordinates' jobs, creating a climate in which your team members are motivated to do their best. Give them meaty projects with decision-making discretion; share information freely; let each team member know their work is an important piece of the overall puzzle. Your objective is to appeal to their intrinsic desire for self-determination and self-expression. (For more information on job motivation, see Chapter 7, where I discuss how you can gain additional insight into your own needs and motives.)

Model the Behavior

This may seem like an obvious point, but plenty of managers stumble here and lose the confidence of their teams. When I say "model the behavior," I mean leading by example in three areas in particular: (1) admitting mistakes and being open to feedback; (2) communicating deliberately and being judicious with the language you use; and (3) varying your managerial style according to the needs of the situation.

We know that one of the only ways for people on your team to improve is by being open to feedback and learning from it. So how can we expect them to have the courage to be open and receptive to constructive criticism if we ourselves are not? To build credibility with your team, there's nothing like admitting to a mistake and then addressing how you're going to rectify it. I talked with former Twitter CEO Dick Costolo about this topic because he is well known for his candor. He said,

> You must be forthright with your team, otherwise you cre-
> ate all kinds of misery for them. I've found that there are
> a lot of managers who have trouble telling it straight with
> their teams. They manage with the goal of wanting to be
> liked and that actually lessens trust. Along the same lines,
> as a manager, it's not your job to be omniscient. If you don't
> know the answer, admit it. I always felt like that attitude fos-
> tered so much trust. They think, "I know Dick is telling it to
> me straight." Overall, it's your job to make sure *they* under-
> stand what *you* understand. You don't have to make all the
> right decisions. It's your job to find the people who can help
> you make the right decisions.

At Walmart, we had a process called a "COE" or "correction of errors." When a person or team really flubbed something, they were expected to create a one-page document that identified the mistake, its impact and ramifications, the reason(s) it happened, and how the person/team was going to ensure it didn't happen again. This information was then presented in front of the affected parties. These mea culpas set a wonderful example of honesty and transparency.

I gave a correction of errors to my fellow Walmart officers and our CEO after the Walmart.com website went down on Black Friday in 2006 because we ran a promotion for the new Tickle Me Elmo doll that increased our site traffic some 400 percent. I was fairly certain I was going to get fired for approving the ill-timed promotion, so on my flight from San Francisco to Bentonville, I read a travel book on Spain, figuring that my wife and I could visit

Barcelona and the south of Spain after I got canned. But I gave a crisp, candid correction of errors where I laid out new methods and procedures we would be using on future promotions to ensure the website could handle a dramatic surge of incremental traffic. Spain would have to wait for another time because that presentation saved me from getting fired, and it was back to work.

In modeling behavior, it's important to pick your words carefully when you communicate with your team. Don't just toss words around. Ask whether you diminish your managerial credibility when you speak:

- Do you waffle and hedge—holding back and then qualifying everything? A few years ago, I asked one of my senior-level vice presidents to note the number of times he said, "I would say the answer is yes and no . . ." and "it really depends . . ." and to watch the look of confusion on his team members' faces as he hedged.
- Do you oversell? Do you overstate your case (drenching your sentences with superlatives like "best of breed" or "world class") or do you push too hard to close the sale, creating commitments you can't keep?
- Are you lazy with language? Do you rely on clichés and acronyms instead of communicating in a more precise or memorable way? How many times have we seen people's eyes roll when the big boss gets up and says a word salad sentence such as, "While we were really impacted by the snow this winter, our best-of-breed TQM solution took us to the next level and was a literal paradigm shift that enabled us to really move the needle with customers."

When modeling behavior, managers get the best results by maintaining a flexible leadership style, strategically using different approaches based on the needs of the business situation. Like a mechanic opening up his toolkit and pulling out the right instrument to solve the task at hand, great managers are able to take the right approach based on the demands of the situation. They are *directive* when the situation is urgent and demands immediate compliance. They are *affiliative* and consensus-oriented when a team is fractured and there's a need to build team harmony and create a sense of shared meaning. They are *visionary* and *inspirational* when the team needs a leader to provide clear direction and give them a shot of confidence. Strong leaders have the ability to examine a situation and ask, "What does this situation require of me?" Sometimes the answer is absolutely nothing—they merely need to be quiet and let the team perform. Other times they need to dive in and change the trajectory of a flailing project.

When I was a twenty-five-year-old manager for PepsiCo's food service division in Canada, I had the opportunity to watch our international division president, Graham "Gill" Butler, demonstrate situational leadership flexibility and it made a strong impression on me. At the time, in November 1988, PepsiCo was still in the restaurant business and owned Pizza Hut and Taco Bell, among other chains. Our Canadian division, which managed both the Pizza Hut and Taco Bell businesses nationwide, was presenting our annual operating plan for the upcoming year to the New York brass, including Gill Butler and his senior staff, who'd flown in the corporate jet from Purchase, New York, to our division office in Toronto to hear our business plan. I was presenting the marketing plan for Taco Bell Canada, and it was the first time I'd presented to any senior leadership team, let alone a PepsiCo division president. I was so nervous that in advance of my presentation, I'd put frames on my acetate slides (remember, this was 1988) to keep them from shaking and rattling when I placed them on the overhead projector.

When it came time to present, I was even more nervous, because the person who preceded me, our director of store operations, took a beating for Taco Bell's prior year's performance, which included a bad combination of low store sales growth and poor quality of service scores. I got through maybe three slides when Butler said in this deep, gravelly voice, "Sit down! SIT DOWN! Just sit down. I don't want to hear any more." He turned to our management team, dressed in grays and blues and seated in the front row. "I have no confidence in your ability to hit this plan. You haven't hit your plan the past two years. I don't want to hear about next year. I want you all to think long and hard about the viability of this business in Canada and come to New York next month with an assessment that proves this business can work. In the meantime, I'm not sinking any more capital in it." Then he stood up, said, "Let's take a short break and then hear from the Pizza Hut team," and walked out of the room. The room sat in stunned silence. Shocked and confused, I turned to our director of operations for assurance. He said, more to himself than to me, "I guess I can always get a job back in commercial real estate." With several sentences, Gill Butler presented us with our stark reality, one that we hadn't been able to admit to ourselves: we were out on Lake Ontario, in a storm, in a leaky vessel. If we couldn't shore it up and prove it could sail, it was going down.

Fifteen minutes later, the Pizza Hut management team presented their business plan. Although I didn't present in that meeting, I was able to attend, because I worked on the Pizza Hut delivery business. Gill Butler sat quietly and listened. Every once in a while, he'd turn to one of his staffers and whisper something, but overall he was very attentive. He asked several thought-provoking questions, which were fielded deftly. Three hours later, the Pizza Hut team presented their final slide. The room was completely quiet. All eyes were on Butler. He stood up and turned to the Pizza Hut management team. He said, "The Seoul Olympics just concluded a few weeks ago. I'd like to congratulate you. You're on your way to a gold medal performance this year. And your operating plan for next year shows that you have no intention of slowing down. I would like to take everyone on the Pizza Hut team out for drinks." The juxtaposition was striking. Butler was a lion at 10:00 a.m. and a panda bear at 4:00 p.m.

Becoming a strong manager and leader is not easy. It can even be counterintuitive. We need to act less assured and be more considered. We need to talk less and listen more. Early in our careers, we're rewarded, like Sarah the Solo Flier was with her promotion, for completing tasks on time and under budget, operating independently, and being decisive within a narrowly defined context of influence (usually the project team or inside our department). Later, however, some of those very strengths can become detrimental when we transition to managing and leading larger teams. For many talented people like Sarah, skilled in and rewarded for "doing," the shift to manager and leader is a hard one. We're required to operate differently, getting work done through others, moving from athlete to coach. We need to move from "me" to "we." It's a challenging shift to make, but essential to succeeding as a manager and leading a team. In Sarah's case, given her intelligence, drive, and willingness to be reflective, the chances are good that she will recover from her shaky start with her new team and move from micromanaging to leading the group.

CHAPTER 3

VERSION 1.0

Inflexible and Dated

Eddy, a successful sales representative for TaskServe Inc., was recently promoted to regional sales manager. TaskServe is a SaaS-based (software as a service) enterprise software company that automates the facilities maintenance process for large retailers like Walgreens or McDonalds. It provides a service that allows thousands of third-party facilities maintenance contractors to seamlessly schedule and complete jobs (such as snow plowing or lawn maintenance) on behalf of retailers and property owners directly through TaskServe's software platform.

Eddy loves selling—being on the road and dealing with customers. As a sales manager, his work has changed but he is still, in his heart, in Version 1.0 of his career, a customer-facing sales rep. Version 1.0s come in many forms—manager, vice president, technical expert, within large or small companies—but they share one characteristic: a reticence to adapt to change. No longer moving to the beat of changing requirements of their work, Version 1.0s throw sand into the company's organizational gears of progress, not to mention their own careers.

Eddy is calling on Julie, the vice president of facilities maintenance for a large home improvement retail chain. One of his sales
reps has had initial conversations with Julie's management team
and this is Eddy's opportunity to land the account. Let's listen in
to understand what afflicts Eddy as he tries to close this new sale.

JULIE: "Eddy, apparently my facilities maintenance team has
had some good initial conversations with your sales reps.
That said, there's an outstanding item that needs to be
answered for me to seriously consider using TaskServe."

EDDY: "I appreciate your time today, Julie, and stand ready
to address your questions so we can work together. I want
to know how we can serve your needs."

JULIE: "Thanks. It came to my attention, only this morning,
that one of your competitors now integrates the work ren-
dered by contract service providers through an interfacing
mobile app, using GPS technology, to instantly validate
and time-stamp all services provided. My team was under
the impression that you don't have this capability. Is that
the case?"

EDDY: "Julie, we have the most robust technology stack of
anybody in the market. We're best of breed and were
rated as such last year, in *TechNow* magazine's client poll
of best SaaS enterprise software products. We can build
any capability that you need—and lightning fast."

JULIE: "Are you saying that you don't have this capability
right now?"

EDDY: "If we don't, I am certain we can build it very quickly
and customize it for your particular needs."

JULIE: "So you don't know if you have the feature?"

EDDY: "I am not quite sure, Julie. I'm pretty sure we don't
quite yet. Let me send out a quick text to confirm, OK?"

JULIE: (sighs as Eddy texts) "OK, while we're waiting, can you tell me, assuming you don't have it, how long would it take to build it and what would it entail?"

EDDY: "Let's do this, Julie: let me dial in one of our technical product managers and see just how fast we can do this for you."

JULIE: "I don't think we have time right now, Eddy. Just tell me—ballpark figure—what it would take to build this interfacing GPS technology into a mobile app for our contractors to use?"

EDDY: "I don't know for sure, Julie, because it's a brand-new technology and I'd hate to give you an inaccurate answer. Let me get right back to you—today—with that answer. If we can build it quickly, I trust we can work together?"

JULIE: "I don't know. We'll see. I'm going to go ahead and meet with the company that currently has this capability— to be up front with you, they're flying in right now from Chicago—and we'll see what they have to offer. But please do get that answer for me and we'll see where this goes."

Julie gave Eddy several chances to make his case and lay out what it would take to develop this new technology in order to get her business. But Eddy was not equipped to answer her question and, as a result, will likely lose the sale. If he had been up to speed on his competitor's technological capabilities, he would not have been caught off guard by Julie's question. As a matter of fact, just two weeks before Eddy's meeting with Julie, at a recent all-hands meeting at TaskServe's Austin headquarters, the company's technical product team provided an update on next year's new product development road map and said that one of the upcoming projects, that would be launched in the third quarter of the year, was the mobile GPS-based software capability that Julie had requested.

But, in that meeting, Eddy, deciding he could bring in the techies when he needed a product update, was sitting in the back of the room and filling out his mounting pile of expense reports and not paying attention to the presentation. Indeed, Eddy not only missed hearing about that vital piece of information, he'd also declined to attend the last two technical product meetings, which were organized so various department managers could be informed of the proposed product development road map and have an influence on TaskServe's future product plans. Why did Eddy miss these meetings? He not only found the technical material mind-numbing, he also saw the crux of his job as being out on the road *selling*—not back in the headquarters discussing the pros and cons of complicated technical product stuff.

Eddy's mistake is typical of people caught in the Version 1.0 syndrome. In his case he not only needs to know the future product development plan but also influence the product road map based on what he and his sales reps are seeing in the competitive marketplace. Eddy also needs to make sure his sales team knows about the company's future product plans—he should be coaching them on how to incorporate new service features into their business pitches.

Version 1.0s may be left behind due to:

- Getting promoted or being rotated to a new assignment with different success criteria;
- Becoming overdependent on a boss or advocate who leaves them at sea when he or she leaves the firm;
- Being fearful of or resistant to inevitable business changes, such as an organizational realignment, or not embracing a shift in the business strategy due to a technological disruption; and

- Lacking in curiosity—being comfortable and wanting things to stay as they are.

The second most common career stopper right behind poor interpersonal skills is difficulty adapting to change. Some research studies state that it affects over half of managers who derailed. As managers rise through organizations, adaptability becomes increasingly important, as business situations become more complex and answers less clear. When we gain additional responsibility, we must deftly manage more constituencies and be aware of a host of political nuances extending from the various departmental agendas of those with whom we work. As executive coach Kevin Murnane said to me, "As you progress in your career, you need to move from the technical to the interpersonal and from certainty to ambiguity."

Tina James, the senior vice president of human resources at top retailer H.E.B., one of the largest private companies in the United States, walked me through the most important personality attributes her company looks for in new hires. As she did so, Tina emphasized exactly what Eddy seemed to lack. She said, "Adaptability is one of the most important traits we talk about at H.E.B. We look for people who are committed to personal growth, are curious, embrace change, and are coachable. It's one of the most important hiring filters for us."

Version 1.0 Material? A Few Questions

Ask yourself the following questions to gain a better understanding of just how open-minded and flexible you are:

- Do you tend to resist change? Is your first reaction to dig in, or to justify the existing game plan?

- Do you look for opportunities to learn new skills and gain new perspectives? How do you do so? What are the ways you "sharpen your saw"?
- Are you up to speed on the latest technologies and trends that are influencing your industry? What are they?
- Do you accept and admit your mistakes and learn from them, or do you seek to justify or hide them?
- What kind of feedback have you received about your adaptability and openness to change? What would those closest to you say?

Difficulty Adapting: Where They Go Wrong

People who lack adaptability often create problems for themselves for three reasons: they're fearful of change, they have a rigid belief system and get stuck in their ways, or they aren't able to adjust to changing circumstances.

Fear of change and the desire to maintain the status quo are common reasons for career trouble, even when people are faced with new business challenges that require a change in approach or developing new skills. They may quietly worry, "I just don't know if I can learn this new approach" and avoid diving in and trying it.

Two of Robert Hogan's eleven dark side personality dimensions (see Chapter 1, page 31) are about people struggling with adapting to change. The first, *cautious*, describes those who are indecisive and risk averse, reluctant to take risks for fear of making mistakes and being negatively evaluated. So they don't act and their very inaction eventually derails them. The second is *dutiful*, those eager to please and reliant on others for support and guidance. They may try to ingratiate themselves to the boss or are reluctant to take independent action that may go against popular opinion for fear of being criticized. As a result, they are seen as lacking backbone by their subordinates and peers and over time lose their respect and support. These derailers often interact with each other. A person's lack of adaptability may, for example, impede his ability to effectively lead a team.

David Dotlich and Peter Cairo, leadership coaches and authors of *Why CEOs Fail*, put it this way: "In our experience, leaders fail when they are routinely and philosophically cautious rather than situationally prudent." By abdicating their very responsibility to make decisions and *manage*, these people instead push paper and create churn, forming committees and recommending further research studies to "illuminate the situation." Risk averse, overly cautious managers clog up the ranks of companies and ensure that nothing substantial gets done. But then, when business results soften, these overly cautious managers often find themselves in positions of vulnerability.

Adya, now the managing director of a large East Coast philanthropic organization, derailed earlier in her career when she became paralyzed by indecision when a new boss entered the picture. "People who adapt well," she told me, "have a sense of 'nonattachment.' It's not that they don't care, it's that they aren't so attached to the old vision or direction or boss that they can't adapt and change. What they have is the flexibility of a tree that bends in the wind." When that new boss came in, Adya said,

> I was so caught up in my job—it was a big part of my identity—and I didn't adapt well to her approach. She had a more aggressive management style, asking for constant updates, managing from a dashboard of core metrics, being very impersonal—and she scared me. I was happy to do all the work but the new measurement methods and how she grilled us on them unnerved me. I had a lot of fear. My lizard brain took over, and rather than working to open the

lines of communication with her, I just hid. When layoffs came around, I was chopped. But I learned from the experience. Now I've become that supple tree that can bend in the wind. When a significant leadership change took place in my next job, and business practices changed with it, I responded with equanimity and I took everything at face value and didn't freeze up. I dealt with the changes head-on. Nothing was an affront to me. I rolled with the changes. And when there were layoffs, I wasn't in there!

*

The familiar can be quite comforting, with things moving smoothly along as they always have. But we run into trouble with a rigid belief system, when we *attach* to an approach or a belief and aren't open to adjusting our mind-set and taking a different approach when compelling new information is presented. Eddy, the TaskServe sales manager, wasn't open to adjusting his mind-set about the role that technology played in his sales job, even in the face of compelling market changes. He might describe himself as a "traditionalist," preferring the orthodoxy of time-tested selling methods, finding the status quo preferable to testing new technologies that could yield unknown results. But when he tried to land a new account with Julie's company, Eddy's lack of interest in understanding his own company's new product road map impeded his ability to answer Julie's question and gain her business. If not addressed, his lack of technical curiosity could hurt his career.

*

There are changing circumstances, usually an inciting incident—a particular event or set of changing circumstances—that lead to an actual derailment, such as going through a job transition, reporting to a new boss, and/or experiencing a fundamental (often technology-driven) industry shift.

When we're transferred into a new job or promoted into a new position we find ourselves having to navigate new terrain and must quickly adapt. After people are promoted, a common theme I've seen and heard is their difficulty in making the mental transition from being an individual contributor to a team manager or moving from a team manager to a department leader. As our work priorities change, our behaviors need to adapt and change as well. In many of these cases, these moves involve a shift from *doing* to *managing* the work and a mind-set shift, of moving from a "me" to a "we" orientation. (I will examine the remedies for this important topic of "job transitions" later.)

A second and very common changing circumstance that can lead to derailment is becoming overdependent on a boss or mentor. When that person is transferred into another position or leaves the firm, we are left without an advocate and become vulnerable. We frequently struggle when we lose our old boss and gain a new one with a different agenda and a different management style, when, say, our former boss was participative and our new one is autocratic. It is common to have difficulty adapting to our new boss's perspective on the business or their leadership style. We must realize that it's incumbent upon us to adapt to them, not them to us.

A key contributor to my getting offtrack for a couple years at Frito-Lay in the mid-1990s was when I went from reporting to a very senior-level boss who worked with me to set my agenda and then backed off, giving me a lot of room to run, to one with a much more hands-on approach to management. Reporting to Mike, a more participative boss, was a new experience for me and I managed him (and our relationship) poorly. In an effort to give myself more room to maneuver, I didn't seek his counsel and failed to update him on the progress of my key initiatives, which only irritated him and resulted in him reeling me in more. From there our relationship went into a downward spiral, as I noted earlier.

A third circumstance that can lead to derailment is difficulty identifying, understanding, and accepting fundamental shifts in the macroenvironment that are affecting our business and then failing to make the necessary adjustments in our jobs. When business strategies change because of competitive marketplace shifts and technological disruptions, we must develop new skills in order to adapt and succeed. For example, with the ubiquity of smart phones, it's becoming increasingly common for shoppers to check prices on retail items before and during their shopping visits. They can find the best price for an item in their shopping area, or, if they don't want to visit a physical store, they can simply price compare and buy the best-priced item online. As a result, retail managers and executives are scrambling to rethink their approach to item-level (SKU, or stock keeping unit) management and pricing strategy. Given shopper price transparency, should retailers be prepared to match or beat prices on competitive items in their store if shoppers find a better price at a nearby store? Should retailers build the capability for shoppers to reserve inventory through their phones prior to visiting their stores? These are strategic questions that have broad ramifications for execution across the retailers' entire business system. How will the leaders of functions such as merchandising, marketing, store operations, logistics, and IT respond to the new world order created by this technological disruption? Will they embrace the change, dig in, conduct research on the new technologies, and immediately start testing new approaches and building adaptive capabilities? Or will they bury their head in the sand, hoping the disruption won't affect their retail business too much?

Another fundamental shift occurs when companies reorganize in order to improve their business performance. It's not uncommon to move from a centralized, "headquarters" reporting structure to a more decentralized, geographically "field-based" structure, or for a company to realign its business from a traditional functional reporting structure to one organized around strategic business units with various functions reporting into specified business units. When this happens, will managers embrace the shift and act as change agents or at the very least be adaptable enough to embrace the new direction?

In the late 1990s, I worked as a vice president of marketing for Electronic Arts (EA), a leading software publisher of video games such as *The Sims, Sim City,* and a well-known franchise of sports games under the name of *EA Sports.* The company was known for the realism of their games—when you play their football game, you feel like you're transported right into the stadium. After I left EA to pursue my own entrepreneurial endeavors, I continued to follow it, watching the company grow from hundreds of millions to billions in revenue. I watched with particular interest to see how EA would respond in 2013, when it became the first company to be twice named the "Worst Company in America" by Consumerist, a high-profile consumer affairs blog owned by a subsidiary of *Consumer Reports* that focuses on consumers' experiences and their issues with companies. Gamers complained they didn't like the way EA did business. These customers complained to Consumerist that instead of releasing new and innovative games, EA fell back on what customers perceived to be cookie-cutter titles that cashed in on well-established series that were, they felt, sloppy, buggy, and half-baked. Gamers also said that EA charged them for small extras and ignored their feedback on what aspects of their games weren't working. Andrew Wilson, who had just come in as CEO, admitted, "We weren't thinking about everything we were doing in the context of the player experience." The days of gamers buying their *EA Sports* disc in a shrink-wrapped box in a retail store and then sitting on the couch and playing their buddies was no longer the norm. Instead, players were buying downloads over the Internet and playing the games online against thousands of challengers around the world. "The company is moving from an offline packaged goods company to an online content delivery service," Wilson said. Because EA hadn't adapted quickly enough to the market shifts and the changing needs of their customers, their stock steadily dropped (falling two-thirds from 2005 to 2012), creating a burning platform for change. Led by Wilson and chairman Larry Probst (one of the people who built EA into one of the world's biggest and most successful video game companies), the company made three key changes.

EA shifted the culture to a "gamer-first" mind-set, emphasizing game quality over quantity and releasing products only when they were polished and "customer-ready." Then by focusing on the high-growth digital channels, especially mobile gaming on iPhone and Android smart phones, and corralling the various business units, EA was able to, as Wilson said, "get to the point where we operate as a single organization." Third, EA shut down several of its game development studios, significantly reduced its workforce, and restructured its business units as part of the strategic changes. A number of previously successful, high-flying managers and executives had trouble adapting to the marketplace changes and EA's new business strategy and ended up leaving or being forced out of the company.

The EA stock price responded very well to the strategic changes, moving from $14 in January 2013 to $72 in December 2015 (as I write this, in mid 2017, it's at $100). CEO Andrew Wilson was named as the number three business person of the year by *Forbes*, behind Nike's Mark Parker and Facebook's Mark Zuckerberg.

Wilson said that EA's comeback was the result of changing the culture to one focused on the EA gamer and less oriented around hitting a game release schedule. "It used to be the entire cadence of the organization revolved around accounting . . . and not the 24/7 rhythm of the digital world." Wilson said the company was a "disconnected organization" made up of well-meaning people who weren't thinking about players—a.k.a. EA's customers—first. Summing up the experience, Wilson said, "I hope we never appear on that list again, I truly do." Chairman Larry Probst later said, "The message I tried to deliver was, 'This will not happen again. As long as I draw breath, this will not happen again.'"

The EA story is a testament to the importance for managers and executives to stay focused on delivering on the needs of the end customer by being adaptable—in this case to the technology-driven marketplace shifts that were taking place as game players moved from offline, console-based game playing to mobile and online games. EA was slow to adapt until Wilson became CEO and provided the burning platform for change. The personnel lay-offs at EA bring to mind a sharp insight of Harry Kraemer, formerly the CEO of Baxter Healthcare and now an executive at private equity firm Madison Dearborn. When stressing the need to be the agent and not the recipient of change, he is known to say, "Are you in the movie or watching the movie?"

Laura Flanagan, the CEO of Foster Farms, the leading poultry producer in the western part of the United States, told me about watching a coworker derail at a company she used to work for because he lacked the skills to learn and adapt to a different work environment:

This person came to our company from one of the top con-sulting firms in the U.S. He was brought in to run one of the divisions of our company. Now, in consulting, the valued product is the presentation deck. You're charged, in the end, to deliver good, sound strategic advice through this format. But that's not the key component to succeeding in a consumer packaged goods environment—it requires a different talent, certainly an ability to develop strategy, but also align resources, enlist teams, and execute programs. But with this person it was *decks, decks, decks.* He presented his ideas to others by standing up and going over his PowerPoint decks instead of working alongside them to build enlistment. Eventually, at one point, he accelerated a product launch without thinking things through and realizing that he needed to check with R&D and with manufacturing to make sure we could make enough of the product. He had years of experience, but he couldn't adapt to the executional nature of our business, and he made this rookie mistake. He didn't last long after that. Not because he wasn't smart—he was. But because he wasn't able to adapt to a new environment—he didn't take the time to ask questions, to watch, listen, and learn so he could understand how to be effective in it.

Six Remedies for Getting Better at Adapting to Change

Remedy #1: Increase Your Learning Agility

Historian Barbara Tuchman, when writing about colossal blunders of political leaders and the narrow-mindedness that gets in the way of sound decision making, observed that "learning from experience is a faculty almost never practiced. 'Wood-headedness,' the source of self-deception, is a factor that plays a remarkably large role in government. It consists of assessing a situation in terms of preconceived fixed notions while ignoring or rejecting any contrary signs. It is acting according to wish while not allowing oneself to be deflected by the facts."

Learning agility—the willingness and ability to learn from experience and apply those lessons to performing well in new and challenging situations—is the solution to "wood-headedness." In a research study that examined more than two thousand managers across all organizational levels to determine whether behaviors associated with managerial effectiveness differed by level, the only factor that was significantly associated with effectiveness at each managerial level was what the researchers call "learning orientation," a combination of learning ability and adaptability. Those who succeeded were quick to absorb information and aggressively sought out knowledge, but they were also flexible enough to accommodate challenges to their knowledge base.

This research was corroborated by two talent development firms—Lominger Limited Inc. and Korn Ferry (the two firms have now merged). Agility in your personal learning—"the subtle skill of picking up on cues and changing one's behavior quickly"—in the words of the Lominger study—is a skill at which all high performers were adept and results in more career promotions. In a ten-year study of managers, Korn Ferry found that the higher an individual's learning agility (which they determined through an assessment), the more career promotions he or she received.

Building and developing learning agility begins with self-awareness, a topic that at this point starts to sound familiar. People with strong learning agility are open-minded and know their true strengths and weaknesses. They understand their biases and where they are too judgmental and can therefore mitigate any tendencies they may have in these directions. Self-awareness is their vehicle for setting personal development goals in order to improve their performance.

Learning-agile people see life and work as a series of ongoing diverse learning experiences. They view failure as situation-specific (not indicative of their ability level) and as an opportunity to learn. So, seek out experiences for purposes of personal growth and development. Accept the responsibility for your own personal and professional development. (See the concluding chapter, "You Can't Count on 'The Man,'" for additional insight.) Try your best to minimize the defenses that inhibit learning—such as fear of disapproval, of being seen as weak, and of being dependent, among others. Seek out that lateral move in your company if it offers you the ability to reignite your learning curve; join that cross functional task force if it gives you visibility into an area with which you have no experience.

A third way to develop learning agility is being action-oriented and taking the initiative to accomplish learning goals. Don't procrastinate when encountering a challenge and put off for tomorrow that which you can address today. Problems don't go away with time; they usually become even more entrenched, so take them on early.

People with learning agility are also reflective, examining their assumptions and methods and critical of their own problem-solving techniques. They attempt to understand unexpected results—why events occurred as they did and what they can learn from those outcomes. They have the ability to examine problems in unusual ways, processing information by integrating patterns, seeing contextual relationships, and connecting seemingly unrelated elements. Often called associational thinking, this ability is a key trait of innovative thinkers. So take the time to stare at the wall and free-associate. And when you're encountering conflict or reflecting on your own performance, do your best to create a little distance from the situation—try to be the participant *and* the observer.

And, remember to stay open-minded. Learning-agile people are interested in hearing new ideas and in discovering new perspectives. They are good listeners, empathetic, and sensitive to cultural differences, and they are willing to adjust their behavior in response to their environment. So try hard to stay flexible, try not to be too judgmental, and don't become locked in to your positions. It's easy to say but very hard to do. I still have to remind myself time and again: "Carter, clear your mind, withhold judgment, and just *listen*." An old boss of mine said, "Most people don't listen; they reload." You don't want to be that gunslinger.

As the senior vice president of global solutions at LinkedIn, Mike Gamson has a unique vantage in understanding how people develop skills and make progress in their careers. "People with great careers," he observes, "are constantly refreshing themselves by reinvesting in their own development. To stay inspired and motivated, they seek out challenges to move beyond the stage they're in now." When I asked Mike about the link between learning agility and career derailment, he said, "People often run into trouble when the role they're in has changed and they have a skill gap they didn't anticipate." Given the revolutionary effect that the Internet and mobile usage has had on consumer buying behavior, Gamson sees the problem coming up in marketing more than any other function. In the past five to ten years, marketing managers and officers have turned over very quickly, he says. "There are," he notes, "those who are social marketing 'natives' and those who aren't. . . . I see people bet on the wrong career skills; they don't invest in the right areas. You must recognize that professional skills have a shelf life—maybe five years max—and if you don't refresh inside of that time frame, you're going to find yourself in real trouble."

Remedy #2: Understand Career Transitions

Difficulty adapting to changing circumstances, especially a job change involving a new assignment or a promotion, can often derail promising careers. People perform well when there is a match between their capabilities and the requirements of their job. When that match gets out of balance, people struggle. While working with both middle- and senior-level managers attending Kellogg School of Management's continuing education program, I've asked hundreds of program participants, "When you were promoted or transferred into a new assignment, how many of you had a clear understanding of the skills required and the success factors of your new job?" Only 10–20 percent of the people raise their hands. Then I've called on people who did raise their hands, asking them how they went about understanding the job requirements and success factors of their new job and trying to create a smooth transition into their new role.

They took one or all of the following actions. First, they took the time to be crystal clear on what their new boss wanted, asking essentially, "What will I have accomplished in two or three years to make you say I did a great job in this role?" From that conversation, they made a list of the three to five key deliverables and then worked with their boss to establish key performance indicators for each. Their goal was to be crystal clear on what success looked like.

Second, if the new boss wasn't able to provide clear direction, they developed their own goals and objectives, with clear success metrics, and then ran them by the boss to ensure alignment.

Third, they sought advice from other employees who had gone through the same or similar transitions, asking about challenges in the transition and what to watch out for. What did they learn? What was more difficult than they estimated? What caught them off guard? In what particular areas did they struggle? Which other departments, functional groups, and resources were critical to their success? What three pieces of advice would they offer?

Then, in the early stages of a job transition, they checked in with the boss on a regular basis—weekly or biweekly. They made sure they were aligned on what was important to accomplish and made sure they received ongoing feedback regarding their performance.

I wish I had taken these steps but the truth is, for a good stretch of my career, I wouldn't have been one to raise my hand and affirm that I had a grip on success criteria in a new job. When I left Frito-Lay and became a vice president of marketing at Electronic Arts, I did not take the time to understand the key deliverables of my new job or the skills and behaviors I needed to learn to be successful in the position. And, as a result, I got off to a slow start, and my tepid midyear performance review reflected it. (Actually, "tepid" is a generous word. I recall my boss, Mark, telling me, "Well, you're off to a slow start here, Carter. The studios [the game developers] don't even know who you are and what you're here to do.") Luckily, he was a good boss and he worked with me to develop a game plan for my new job. That started with getting out of the headquarters office and visiting the field studios that made our games, such as *Sim City* and our other *EA Sports* video games. During these visits I asked how I could assist them in making even better games and then marketing them more effectively. I learned that my number one priority should be to help the game studios by developing a scalable user research method to test various products in the beta stage of development and learn what our target audience thought of them. What needed to be changed to get the game ready for release? Before my field trips, developing a scalable beta-stage user research program wasn't one of the job priorities I'd identified. It became one and my next performance review went much better than the previous one.

It's important to realize that job requirements shift with each career move we make. With each job transition, our mind-set and, at times, our very self-conception must change and adapt to a new set of circumstances. In *Leadership Passages*, author David Dotlich and his colleagues say, "Learning from a passage isn't possible unless you let go of your past assumptions. In other words, you must admit that some of the very attributes, qualities, attitudes and skills that made you successful in the past won't necessarily make you successful in the future."

There are at least four significant management transitions that we go through when progressing in our careers. In order to be adaptable and avoid the Version 1.0 syndrome, determine those particularly relevant to your next job, and take the time to map out your game plan to ensure you understand the new job requirements.

Shift #1, from Managing Self to Managing Others

This shift is the transition—the shift in thinking and the change in behavior—that Sarah the Solo Flier needs to embrace to become a successful manager. She must shift from being a "doer" to planning

Key Management Transitions

Managing Self to Others	Managing Others to Functions	Managing Functions to Businesses	Managing Businesses to Enterprises
1	2	3	4
Accomplishing Through Others	**Becoming Strategic**	**Leading and Integrating**	**Inspiring and Enlisting Others**
Shift from doing to managing	Communicate effectively	Gain alignment	Establish a compelling vision
Plan the work	Secure resources	Ask the right questions and listen carefully	Prioritize the work
Coach others	Be both strategic and tactical	Manage under conditions of uncertainty	Build strong constituencies and manage them

the work and managing through others and coaching and enabling the team versus micromanaging the team.

Shift #2, from Managing Others to Managing Functions

This shift is also a challenging transition. As job scope and responsibilities broaden significantly it becomes important to think strategically about driving business results and to make sure our team works effectively with other functional groups to accomplish departmental goals. If we don't want to become a Version 1.0, with our broadened set of accountabilities, we must be adaptable in at least three areas. First, we must communicate effectively at least two levels down into our organizations—to our direct reports and also, in various departmental meetings, to their direct reports. We not only need to clearly and constantly communicate our team priorities but also take the time to explain how they fit in to the context of the company's overall business strategy. Second, it's critical that we be able to secure needed resources for our team— whether it's funding or support from other functional groups—so they can execute on departmental priorities. Third, we must learn to be, simultaneously, strategic and tactical. We must be able to zoom in and pull back, to think both broadly about what to do to drive results and tactically about how to do it.

Shift #3, from Managing Functions to Managing Business Units

This shift is often a rewarding passage. We have more autonomy to make decisions and we can clearly link our efforts to marketplace results. Nonetheless, when we manage a discrete business unit, there are at least three broad areas that are different from managing a department or function—where we must learn and adapt. First, we must align and coordinate the various business activities within the different functions for which we are accountable—from procurement to logistics to marketing and selling—in order to deliver on our overall business strategies. Second, we must listen well and ask smart questions. We are now managing people who have expertise in areas we do not, so we need to seek their counsel and remain open-minded regarding their proposed solutions to problems. Third, we must realize that we're managing under conditions of uncertainty. We must learn to become comfortable navigating unknown waters where the business problems are more nuanced and the answers aren't always clear.

Shift #4, from Managing Businesses to Managing Enterprises

With this shift, we become even more focused on inspiring and enlisting others, setting a clear direction and modeling key values through our behavior. There are several areas where we must be adaptable. First, we must establish a compelling vision, engaging our team in creating it and then communicating it in a compelling way, rich with stories and examples to make it come to life. At its very best, this is a vision that entices others to come along on the journey, tapping into a dormant collective aspiration inside our people—something they would be proud to come in to work every day to pursue: to democratize the skies like Herb Kelleher at Southwest Airlines; to inspire the athlete in each one of us like Phil Knight at Nike; to help people save money so they can live better like Sam Walton at Walmart. Second, we must be able to prioritize the work. All great leaders have the ability to determine the strategic direction, to make hard choices and decide what needs to get done amid a sea of competing priorities. We need to identify the right hill to take and to make sure that goals and objectives up and down the organization line up with owners and success metrics. Third, we need to learn to be savvy in building strong constituencies and managing them effectively, from buyers, suppliers, and customers to financial analysts and members of the media. It's a never-ending challenge to manage key constituents while staying plugged in to the core operational aspects of the business. Last, we need to always remember we're only as good as our team members, so we must spend much of our time building and then developing a championship team, from mentoring high-potential managers to recruiting new talent into the company to going on the road and selling the company vision to others.

In order to succeed in a job transition, you need to be prepared to question, even let go of some of the old traits and behaviors that made you successful in your previous job. That's *hard*—some traits and behaviors may have served you well in the past but may not serve you well in the future—behaviors like diving in to do the work yourself instead of delegating to your team, or spending an undue amount of time inside the four walls of the headquarters instead of traveling out in the field, learning from and communicating with suppliers, buyers, customers, and your sales force.

This is tough stuff! It requires reflection and deliberation to determine the skills and behaviors that no longer serve you well, to understand the requirements of your new position, and then to be willing to evolve and change.

Remedy #3: Become More Approachable

Some people's fear of change can be masked as assured arrogance or by being a contrarian. In the first case, like Madonna, they "strike a pose." They protect themselves by being rigid and aloof and acting with complete assurance. Then, when challenged with a contrary point of view, they become combative and aggressive, like Captain Fantastic. As a result, they build an emotional moat around themselves and people can't reach them. Their arrogance leads to a dangerous lack of approachability and eventually they find themselves out of the commercial flow of their organization and emotionally distanced from coworkers. The best antidote I've found to fear-based arrogance is, oddly enough, showing vulnerability. If you've received feedback that you're not approachable, the next time you're in a meeting and there's a point of contention, when it's your turn to weigh in, say, "I don't know. This one's a doozy. What do you guys think? I'm all ears." First, watch jaws drop open. Second, watch a few of them offer a tentative smile. Third, listen for the increased flow of conversation.

In the second case, you have the contrarian, whose favorite response to any challenge or proposed change is *"yeah-but."* When someone says, "Perhaps we should consider testing an artificial intelligence administrative assistant, given how inexpensive it is," the contrarian says, "Yeah-but it's creepy—and management will never go for it anyway." We don't want to be that person—the one who resists every change when it comes knocking at his door. He eventually gets a reputation for being so opposing and resistant that people stop running ideas by him and providing him with any sort of feedback.

If you think you've burned bridges because of lack of approachability, identify those people who've distanced themselves from you and approach them with a good old-fashioned mea culpa. When you apologize: be direct; show vulnerability; shut up, listen, and don't justify your past behavior. For example, you might say, "I haven't been listening to you. I've resisted your ideas. You deserve better. I'm sorry. Can we do a reset? Would you be kind enough to lay out your point of view again? I'm going to just shut up and listen to you."

Remedy #4: Break Out of Your Comfort Zone

People often have difficulty adapting because they've become stuck in their comfort zone, relying on the tried and true. They stop pushing themselves. They stop seeking new experiences and sources of inspiration. In my experience, the first trick to breaking free is to recognize that you're in a rut, which isn't always easy. Inertia is a powerful force. To break free of this tendency toward stasis, I ask myself the following questions:

- *In my current position, what is my "learn/leverage" ratio— what percentage of the time am I learning new skills and gaining new perspectives versus leveraging the skills and tools I already know?* In my early thirties, I wanted that learn/leverage ratio to be about 70/30. But even now, in my fifties, I strive to have that ratio be somewhere round 40/60. In other words, even though it's my job to teach students and counsel entrepreneurs, I still want, in the course of a week or month, to be learning new skills and tools at least 40 percent of the time.

- *What have I learned this week?* The best way I know to capture knowledge is by journaling—and then periodically examining, synthesizing, and applying what I've written. My journals are full of observations, notes from books I've read, mistakes and what I've learned from them, quotes and great ideas from other people, and idea fragments of areas I want to pursue in the future.

- *What can I do to push myself out of my comfort zone this week?* Can I become an early adopter of some new technology and push myself to understand it? (Perhaps I should buy an IoT [Internet of Things] device and wrestle with it.) What new experience can I have to challenge myself this week? Perhaps I should sign up to lead the United Way campaign for my office. Maybe I should build my own website and start to blog. Perhaps I should leave early and walk or ride my bike to work and observe my surroundings a bit more closely. We all get into a rut. Find ways to mix things up and get out of it.

Remedy #5: Fight against Perfectionism

"Perfect," Voltaire said, "is the enemy of good." In their desire for assurance ("I want to be 100% sure this is the right solution before I proceed"), it's common for perfectionists to continue gathering data and running tests in order to make a risk-free decision. But their risk avoidance is, in reality, decision avoidance. Their desire for certainty paralyzes them, especially in ambiguous situations, and leads to inaction. My own tendency toward perfectionism comes in the form of wanting to polish and polish a new idea or a new product instead of getting a minimum viable product (MVP) out into a test market to see how it performs. To fight this tendency, I ask myself:

- "What's the worst thing that can happen if I do this? Is that an acceptable risk?" And I compare that to the risk of *not* doing it. Often, the risk of avoidance is worse.
- "How can I deconstruct the risk, separating reversible from irreversible decisions?" If this decision is ultimately reversible, then let's go! If it's not, I need to be careful and make sure I have answers to the right questions.

Remedy #6: Expand Your Constituency Base

One-third of the one hundred managers I surveyed cited a lack of mentorship as an important reason for their derailment. A change occurred in their company (often a reorganization that led to a new boss) and they found themselves on uneven footing—trying to understand a new set of business priorities and trying to become credible with the new sheriff in town. One man I spoke to described it as being "on the outside looking for hooks to get back inside." At times like these, when organizational circumstances change, it's important to have a broad constituency base to tap in to—to seek advice and at times to even use for safe harbor. For example, in my midthirties I was at Frito-Lay in a trade marketing job in the West Coast, calling on key supermarket and grocery accounts like Safeway and Fred Meyer. One day I came into the office to find a lot of hallway whispering and closed-door sessions. I learned that the company was reorganizing and in the restructuring process, Frito-Lay was going to completely dismantle the West Coast office. My job? "Going away, same as mine," said my boss. I went into my little office, dialed up the vice president of marketing, a mentor of mine out of our Dallas headquarters, and asked if he needed any help. A few weeks later I was living in Dallas, working in his organization. The lesson: take the time to develop strong relationships, both laterally and with key influencers higher in your organization! The chances are just about 100 percent that you'll need their help at some point. Part and parcel to this: be careful not to rely excessively on one boss or advocate. Cast your fishing line into multiple water holes. It's not uncommon for a person to become overdependent on a boss—then the boss leaves or is transferred to another division and you're all alone. Or you may find yourself in the position where your boss is overreliant on you and doesn't put you up for other jobs because they so appreciate what you do for them. One way to think about this is to ask yourself if you have a distinct identity that's separate from your boss's. Do others question if you could perform well without the boss? If the answer is "yes" it's time to break free or expand your base.

Will Eddy, our sales manager from TaskServe, become an ossified Version 1.0 or will he embrace some of these remedies and become more adaptable? He clearly needs to address his lack of interest in—or innate resistance to—new software technologies and instead of ignoring them, study and be conversant in them to aid his selling efforts. Perhaps losing a few new business pitches because he's unable to respond to technical questions and requests will be the catalyst for Eddy to wake up. Or perhaps a watchful boss will notice Eddy's lack of attendance in the company's software development meetings and will help him realize that he needs to have a sufficient understanding of the technical features of their product. Either way, if the trend continues as is, Eddy will receive some sort of wake-up call. Hopefully, it'll come sooner rather than later, before there's damage to his career.

CHAPTER 4

THE ONE-TRICK PONY

Mind the (Skill) Gap

Gail Ross has been the financial controller of Warm Hearth ("Smell the Goodness"), a midsized company that makes cookies and other baked goods sold through grocers and supermarkets throughout the western United States, for the past five years. She's a talented forty-year-old numbers whiz and now has her eye on the prize of becoming a chief financial officer.

After finishing the annual performance review with her boss, Ron, the CFO, Gail walks back to her office, shuts the door, drops a manila file folder on her desk, and sits down heavily in her chair. She gives a long exhale. Most of the review went well, with an "above target" rating and a salary increase well above the company average. But she is deflated and irked. Gail leans back in her chair and reflects. She knew she was good at her job; no one could doubt that ever since she'd become the controller at Warm Hearth, the company's financial management execution—and their financial health—had dramatically improved. Under her leadership and because of her skillful understanding of accounting and cash flow management, the company put in place a comprehensive set of controls and budgeting processes designed to mitigate risk, enhance the accuracy of their reported financial results, and ensure that their reports complied with generally accepted accounting principles and financial reporting standards. Basically, the place was running like a well-oiled machine.

Gail stared at the manila folder containing her performance review. Why, in the development section of the review, under "future role," didn't it say "chief financial officer"? Instead, it read in irritating corporate-speak, "Performing with Excellence," code for "Hold in Place."

The answer she had received thirty minutes ago, when she'd asked Ron about her path to a promotion, was still swimming around in her brain. He had said, "Gail, you're in your sweet spot. You're doing your job really well. It's what you're meant to do." Annoyed by his presumptuous response, she had retorted, "I don't need you to tell me what I'm meant to do, Ron. It's up to me to determine what I'm meant to do." He had replied, "Actually, it's not—not while you're here, anyway. The company decides that."

After they'd both calmed down, they discussed why she wasn't being considered, down the road, for his job. Ron gave her three reasons. First, he said, although she was incredibly skilled at all things accounting and could sniff out an aberrant financial allocation from miles away, she had meaningful gaps in "other pertinent areas of strategic corporate finance management," such as long-range strategic planning and business forecasting, which he said were crucial aspects of a CFO's skill set. Second, she was so focused on executing her priorities that she was one-dimensional— for example, he said, she had never taken the time to understand the key drivers of business performance in other departments, like marketing and account sales. She didn't know, he said, "what

propelled the business forward and how all the pieces fit together."
He summarized by saying that it all boiled down to her having
"signature strengths, but a lopsided skill profile."

Gail, exasperated that Ron had only *now* brought this massive
issue to her attention, swept the manila folder onto the floor with
a brush of her hand and settled back in her chair to consider her
next move.

If Ron is indeed correct, Gail is a "one-trick pony," overly reliant on a single, signature skill—in her case, financial accounting.
She has not sufficiently broadened her financial management
skill set and she lacks a broader, strategic perspective on the business that would allow her to achieve her goal of becoming the CFO.

One-Trick Ponies are at risk of experiencing career trouble due to:

- Getting mired in the details associated with their signature skill
  area and having trouble seeing the big picture beyond their
  area of expertise;
- Not seeking out broadening assignments—not taking lateral moves into other departments to increase their business
  knowledge;
- Not having a strategic orientation—being unable to identify
  and prioritize the most important activities that drive value for
  their department or company;
- Getting overwhelmed by business complexity and struggling
  when working on projects outside of their specific domain
  area knowledge; and
- Having a skill or knowledge gap in a key area of the business that drives enterprise value (such as store operations
  for a retailer or software development for a technology
  company).

Gail is ambitious and wants to move to the next level. But even people who love what they're doing and aren't gunning for the next position up the ladder should still be watchful of becoming so specialized that they have difficulty connecting the dots and establishing the important linkages between their job tasks and those of adjacent positions or departments. Not doing so can reduce their current job effectiveness because they don't understand the areas in which their own work is dependent on the work of other groups. For example, say you're a marketer who specializes in search engine marketing and is responsible for building keyword campaigns to drive consumers to your website. To be effective in your job you'll need to have an understanding of the work done by the user experience and design team, as they are likely the group who will build landing pages for the consumers that click on your keywords. Generally speaking, it's not enough to know how to do your job really well—you must also have a sound understanding of the key tasks of the adjacent departments on which you have dependencies.

Got Strategic Orientation?

See whether you're at risk of becoming a One-Trick Pony by asking these questions about breadth of knowledge and strategic orientation:

- Do you nearly always rely on your signature skill when facing a business challenge? Do you find that you approach problems the same way, using a similar formula, or are you able to examine business issues from the perspective of other key constituents because you understand how their jobs function?

- Have you focused on one type of work, holding similar positions throughout your career, or have you taken lateral moves that have broadened your business perspective?
- Do you tend to avoid accepting or asking for assignments that would push you into areas where your skills are untested?
- Is there an evident gap in your skill set, one that doesn't allow you to really understand how all the pieces fit together in your company? If so, what skills does your boss say are important for you to learn to gain a broader organizational perspective?
- Have you received feedback that you're so detail oriented that you're myopic and need to pull back and consider the big picture, looking at the marketplace dynamics surrounding your company and the activities of your key competitors?

Where They Go Wrong

One-Trick Ponies who lack strategic orientation usually run into trouble for three reasons: becoming overdependent on a single skill, having a key skill deficiency in an important area of the business, and being viewed as "nonstrategic."

*

Strengths can have unintended consequences when overapplied. The old adage "If all you have is a hammer, everything looks like a nail" comes to mind—for example, a finance manager trying to pin a return on investment to all projects, even those that are exploratory or conceptual, or an advertising agency creative director focusing on the subtle design aesthetics of a client's advertisement at the expense of making the message clear and compelling to the buying public. It's hard to move beyond the core skills that have been serving us well. Research by Hay Group, a global consulting and talent development firm, points to experiential and skill set "narrowness" as a critical career derailer, where workers suffer from taking a "short-sighted emphasis on immediate results and/or technical expertise" instead of taking lateral assignments that will broaden their perspective.

Leadership researchers Lombardo and Eichinger put it this way in their book *FYI: For Your Improvement*: "One of the requirements for higher-level management and career fulfillment is broadness and diversity. A single skill is never enough." This single-minded orientation eventually derails the careers of talented people.

That was the case with Aaron, the chief technology officer in a software services company whose career stalled because he lacked an understanding and interest in any initiative taking place outside of the technology space. During executive committee meetings with the CEO and the rest of the C-suite staff, Aaron didn't contribute to the dialogue. He would sit at the conference room table, tapping away on his laptop, working through his own agenda items. His CEO said,

> For anything not related to building software or hardware infrastructure, he'd tune out or he'd say, "Just tell me what you want me to do." He said that all the time and it drove me nuts. I'd say, "Come on, talk to me! Tell me what you think!" And I'd get nothing. He just wanted to do his job. That's it. Nothing beyond it. I had to kick him off the executive committee and eventually—even though he was quite good at software development—I realized he wasn't the CTO I needed. I needed someone who had a perspective on and interest in the rest of the business—who thought beyond the specific projects under their jurisdiction.

Contrast Aaron with Brock Leach, who looked for opportunities to broaden his scope throughout his career. Brock, now an ordained minister for the Unitarian Church, was, earlier in his career, the president and CEO of Frito-Lay North America and then the CEO of Tropicana. Brock's path to the presidency of Frito-Lay was anything but narrow. He started out as an assistant product manager on the Lays potato chip brand, then moved out to the field, where he was a zone trade marketing manager. In that position, Brock learned how to activate corporate-driven marketing programs at the retail level, using trade marketing dollars to pitch for additional shelf space. Armed with this knowledge, he came back into Frito-Lay headquarters as a director of marketing for the potato chip brands (including Lays and Ruffles). Then, after a few years, he moved back out into the field, where he eventually became a vice president and general manager of the New England area. There Brock learned nearly all aspects of the business, from manufacturing to product distribution to route- and account-level sales. Then he moved back into the headquarters as the vice president of marketing. Just four years later, he was tapped to be the president and CEO of Frito-Lay North America. When Brock reflected on why he was tapped for the CEO position, his insights point to the importance of taking broadening assignments to provide career optionality and avoid becoming pigeonholed into doing one job over and over and hitting a premature career ceiling. Brock said, "I wasn't thinking about my career in linear terms. I took whatever opportunity increased my learning. I was willing to take advantage of opportunities that other people thought would take them off their career track, such as moving out into field roles that weren't close to the headquarter power base. Eventually, I ended up with a unique set of experiences that no one else had." Brock's field sales, trade marketing, and manufacturing rotations gave him a broad, holistic perspective on the business that allowed him to have good business judgment when he ran the entire marketing function and later the entire US business. He knew the right questions to ask when Frito-Lay marketers such as myself were wrestling with whether to invest in the capital expense of retooling the manufacturing plants to produce Tostitos Scoops; he knew how to lead the company with a competitive response plan when rival Nabisco announced it was moving into Frito-Lay's turf, the salty snack business.

Was Brock worried about getting offtrack by moving out of headquarters—that he'd get "lost" out in the field and lose touch with his corporate advocates? "I do think it's important to have someone advocating for you when you take one of those lateral moves," Brock said. "I had an advocate or two who I felt were looking out for me. But I think that sooner or later, if you solve problems, people will recognize it and want you to work with them. For people who are overly focused on their titles and their progression, I'd say 'It's fine and good to be ambitious, but more than anything you want to accomplish things and establish a track record.' The good people always say, 'What else can I do for you? What else can I take on for you?'"

*

A skill gap in a critical area of business—for example, not understanding the technology behind a software product or the enterprise selling process in a business-to-business services company—can impede managers trying to progress in their careers. This is particularly true for those who lack a fundamental understanding of their company's key "critical path" activities or functions. In project management, critical path describes the tasks that must start and finish on time to ensure that the project is completed on schedule. However, I use this concept more broadly to describe *the key functions and activities inside a company that improve the customer experience and drive sales.* In this context, the critical path is the most important set of activities in a firm's value chain, which, when executed well, result in delighted customers and a thriving business. For example, at Walmart, key critical path activities include sourcing and buying products (with a great price-to-value ratio), supply-chain logistics (getting products into consumers' hands at the lowest possible cost), and store operations (clean, well-lit stores with easy-to-find products and the ability to check out quickly). Ascendant managers at Walmart would find that the lack of a fundamental understanding of these three areas (merchandising, distribution/logistics, or store operations) eventually will impede their career progress at the company. It's no surprise that the past three CEOs at Walmart came from the logistics or merchandising functions but also rotated through other departments, such as store operations, to ensure they had a good working understanding of key revenue-generating functions.

When I was the vice president of marketing at Walmart.com my boss, the CEO, told me during one of my performance appraisals, "If you ever want to be considered for my job, you'll have to expand your skills beyond marketing and get into either merchandising or operations." So I spent the next several years in merchandising. And then, most likely as a result of gaining this essential experience, I was promoted to president and later to CEO.

How do you identify your company's critical path areas? Here are some ways:

- Can you name the key success metrics at your company—the ones in the weekly financial flash reports; the ones the CEO and senior management teams track and talk about in their update meetings? Which functions are accountable for those key metrics? The chances are good that they are critical path functions.

- Follow the money. Which departments and teams are well funded? Where are the financial and people resources being invested? On the flip side, what groups or activities are the first to be chopped in the middle of the third quarter during a tough year? Those are *not* critical path activities.
- Which departments generate the most top leaders? At EA, it was the game developers—the executive producers and the software designers. During my time at EA, I had a pivotal discussion with one of the legends of the company, Bing Gordon, one of a handful of people who built it into a powerhouse. After I'd been at EA for a year or so, Bing said to me, "If you want to go places around here, you better dig in to the product and understand game play—what makes a good game good and a bad game bad. You should do a rotation out into one of our studios. You have the marketing skills but not the gaming skills." Realizing that I had no interest in spending my evenings learning about game play or working in one of the game-development studios, I left the company within the year.
- In all-hands meetings and in other key business presentations, which departments and activities get the most airtime? When I was at Pizza Hut, the store operations folks were usually on stage giving the key presentations; when I was at Frito-Lay, it was the field sales people; at the Kellogg School of Management, it's the tenured faculty members.

*

More than once I've heard a senior executive say, "I really like Larry, but I'm just not sure he's *strategic*." I heard it about myself in a performance review when I was in my early thirties. "Carter, you're good at getting things done, but management isn't sure you're *strategic*." Who is "management" and what does "strategic" mean? The boss can be quite vague on this topic. How can we address something so ill-defined and indistinct? Over time, I've learned when "management" says a person is "nonstrategic" they usually mean one of three things:

- Being a whirlwind of execution, getting lost in the weeds of daily and weekly tasks, and not pulling back to examine and understand the strategic context surrounding the work. At Walmart.com, I frequently urged my team to remember to "zoom in and pull back; zoom in and pull back"—to learn to be adept at focusing both on the details and the strategy behind them.
- Being too technically oriented: becoming so absorbed in the "what"—the science or technological capabilities behind a product or system—that you lose your perspective on the "why" behind it.
- Lacking a holistic understanding of how the pieces of the business fit together by not grasping the company's value chain—the process or activities by which a company adds consumer/customer value—and not having an integrated understanding of the macro ecosystem in which the business operates. This would include gaining a fundamental understanding of your industry (the relevant political, economic, societal, and technological trends inside it), the competitive environment in which you compete (determining which competitors are gaining traction and why, understanding where they are vulnerable, determining where there might be "white space" opportunities for the firm), and the role and power of buyers and suppliers. (I'll dig in to this topic in the next section, "Becoming More Strategic.")

Ironically, being nonstrategic can be traced back to being promoted too quickly, where organizations unwittingly play a complicit role. Firms, in an effort to fill the widening talent gap, move talented managers too rapidly through key assignments (and do not offer lateral moves that will increase their exposure and perspective) and also forgive those managers' poor interpersonal behaviors if they achieve short-term results.

In my PepsiCo years, I observed many cases of this "shooting-star syndrome." Very talented managers came charging through the ranks, lobbying for promotions, and moving quickly up the ladder to the level of vice president or even senior vice president, only to flame out as a result of either hubris or the lack of experience to tackle broad, difficult, multifaceted assignments that required a sound understanding of the work that went on inside various departments.

Brock Leach, the CEO turned minister, told me about an ambitious sales and marketing executive who flamed out for this very reason:

> This fellow was very ambitious. He was constantly angling to get himself in positions that he perceived to be good for his career trajectory. But he didn't put his head down and get results—he was too busy watching out for his career. Eventually he was put in this big generalist job that required integrative thinking. He didn't have enough experience to know how to evaluate the best path forward in situations that involved multiple constituents with competing interests. He'd never managed a diverse group before. In under a year, it was obvious to all that he was stumped. He was moved to a smaller job. The guy was overly focused on getting to the next level.

Mike Luecht is the chief executive officer of ML Realty Partners, an industrial real estate investment firm in the central United States. Mike, a talented entrepreneur (he was inducted into the Chicago Entrepreneurial Hall of Fame in 2014), founded the firm in 2001. The derailer he sees most frequently—no surprise by now—is poor interpersonal skills, specifically a lack of self-awareness. Mike said, "You can start believing your own crap and become blind to your blind spots. A recurring theme in the commercial real estate business is that the best transactional people are terrible organizational leaders. They can't get thirty people to follow them up the hill." That derailer is followed, says Mike, by a lack of strategic orientation:

> I've seen it time and again—the most brilliant deal makers get promoted to chief operating officer and move to headquarters. They're good at one thing—really good—but they don't get the big picture. They're tactically strong at closing deals but don't have vision, and they can't think out ahead of the present. You have to be aware of what I call the "fourth chess move." I ask people to play out this scenario with me: "What's the third or fourth chess move you're going to make to build longer-term market share? Or what are the steps you're planning to succeed in a protracted negotiation?" You can't get to the "take" move too quickly. That key move—the "ask" you've slowly been building up to—could take months or even years to set up! You'd think the most aggressive people get to the desired outcome, but it's usually the opposite. The thoughtful people—those not hell-bent on hitting their quota but instead thinking out ahead and developing strong marketplace relations—they are the ones who usually get ahead. So I try to work with people on thinking about their

desired outcomes—then going four moves out and working backwards as to how to get there.

Becoming More Strategic

How does a person like Gail, a skilled controller, but a One-Trick Pony, broaden her capabilities and improve her strategic thinking to get on the path of landing the job of chief financial officer? Here are ten perspective-broadening ways that can improve strategic acumen.

Conduct a Value Chain Right-to-Succeed Exercise

To help broaden the strategic perspective of members on my team, one exercise I do is ask them to lay out, on a whiteboard, the key aspects of our company's value chain (the series of activities by which we build consumer/customer value) and then consider which activities are our company's source of differentiation and drive its success in the market. At Frito-Lay, for example, the value chain would consist of:

- Ingredient and material sourcing
- Manufacturing
- Supply chain distribution
- Marketing
- Route and account selling
- Customer service

Underneath each value chain component, I'd ask them to list the most important activities that the company carries out—the ones that most differentiate the firm from the competition. I would usually lend assistance on this part of the exercise. For example, under "marketing" they would probably list two areas in particular: (1) developing integrated brand and trade marketing campaigns that increase retail shelf space and increase on-shelf product turn rates, and (2) developing great-tasting, consumer-preferred new products that drive incremental sales.

Then, I would say, "OK, of all the activities that have been listed in each area of the value chain, which are absolutely critical for the company to do really well? Which activities give the company a real right to succeed in the marketplace?" In the case of Frito-Lay, a sales- and marketing-driven company, they are activities like "developing great-tasting new products that drive incremental sales" and "developing and selling in trade sales programs that garner incremental retail shelf space."

This exercise is a great way for team members to gain a more holistic perspective on their organization's business. And by thinking through the sequence of key activities that create value for their company, workers can better familiarize themselves with those differentiating activities and understand where their own work fits in to the company's critical work flow.

Conduct a Competitive Marketplace Analysis

I often encourage my team members to examine the marketplace by doing a competitive marketplace "5 Cs Analysis." This exercise would help Gail to think about external factors that affect the future success of her Warm Hearth cookie company. It works well as a group exercise. When I conduct one with my team, I ask them to write down five headings:

- *Category* (the various components and factors influencing the industry itself, including macrofactors like economic conditions, technological changes, as well as the growing or waning influence of buyers, suppliers, and other key constituents, such as strategic partners);

- *Competition* (not only the key reference competitors but also competitive substitutes—where the company's end users would spend their dollars if they bought products or services outside of industry categories);
- *Customers* (for example, clients or key accounts in the company's trade channels);
- *Consumers* (the end users); and
- *Company* (the firm itself).

Then, under each of these five "C" headings, we would discuss the relevant political, economic, societal, and technological factors (an acronym referred to as "PEST") that were aiding, hurting, or might threaten the future health of our business. The chances are pretty good that after having several diligent working sessions, going through this exercise as well as the previous value chain one, anyone who suffered from being called "nonstrategic" would be well on the road to shedding the moniker.

Think Outside-In, Not Inside-Out

People with a strong strategic orientation approach problems from an "outside-in" perspective. When facing a problem, such as increasing customer demand for a product with declining volume, they start by examining the external factors that are outside the four walls of their firm; they don't start by trying to identify product-related issues and fixing them. People who are strong "outside-in" thinkers begin with the external factors, such as marketplace changes in buyer behavior, customers' current path to purchase and buying experience, issues their clients are facing, suppliers' problems, a technological disruption that's creating change and uncertainty, and so on. Then they examine how these factors are affecting the overall customer demand characteristics of their product/service. Only then do they focus inside their firm and examine internal issues. The outside-in approach is guided by the belief that success comes from understanding the sources of customer value creation, which is based on having a customer orientation and understanding the entire customer experience and the context in which they are buying.

An example of how an inside-out approach can get you in trouble when it comes to business strategy took place in the midnineties when I was still at Frito-Lay. At that time, our company made a push beyond salty snacks to enter a new category—snack cakes, with products such as Oatmeal Creme Pies, Swiss Cake Rolls, and Honey Buns. Frito-Lay, the thinking went, would take advantage of the massive distribution power of its sales force to power into the snack cake category. Frito-Lay's management felt their existing brands wouldn't extend to snack cakes (Doritos Snack Cakes doesn't seem very compelling, does it?) so they created a joint venture partnership with bakery powerhouse Sara Lee. They'd work with Sara Lee to develop a line of snack cakes, branded under the Sara Lee name, and then Frito-Lay would distribute them to convenience and gas stores across the United States. Frito-Lay's strategic thought process went something like this: "Sara Lee is a great brand name; we have the world's best sales distribution network; our thirteen thousand route sales people already call on these convenience and gas store accounts multiple times per week; we can garner incremental sales by adding these snack cakes on our route trucks."

From an internal Frito-Lay perspective, it seemed like a great idea, but there was one little problem. They didn't ask consumers if they needed a new line of snack cakes. Hostess already had a line of snack cakes, such as Twinkies, and they would prove to be a formidable competitor, acting aggressively to protect their turf.

Furthermore, it turned out that consumers just loved Little Debbie snack cakes and thought, with their single-serve packaged products priced as low as a quarter, they offered tremendous value for the money. Nonetheless, in 1996, Frito-Lay and Sara Lee launched the new venture, Sara Lee Breakaways, a line of snack cakes priced at eighty-nine cents. The new venture launched in the southeast United States and included cupcakes, Danishes, brownies, muffins, and even an iced pound cake and fat-free cereal bars.

I talked to a former Frito-Lay manager who worked on the launch, and was told:

> Frito-Lay wanted to expand its revenue base by getting into a new part of the day—breakfast—where we weren't represented. We thought, "We're great distributors. This is a big category. Let's go in and take a pound of flesh from the main player, Hostess." So we created our own version of their product line—we basically mimicked them. We did try to emphasize product freshness in our marketing and selling— that with our powerful route sales network, we could get the baked goods into retail stores faster than our competitors, but that distinction wasn't really relevant to consumers. The problem with the whole project was we didn't do a thorough market analysis to see if there was a customer need or a competitive white space that wasn't being served. We just knew we had a great big sales force and we figured our distribution muscle would get us market penetration. It turned out that wasn't enough and the project was shuttered pretty quickly.

Determine Your Skill Gaps and Build a Bridge

If I was working with Gail, the controller at Warm Hearth, the first thing I would recommend she do is to pinpoint her skill gaps as they relate to the chief financial officer position she desires. What are the job requirements of the CFO position, and how do they match her current abilities? Where does she have skill gaps? During Gail's performance review, Ron, her boss, mentioned that she had little experience in long-range strategic planning and business-level forecasting. What projects can Gail undertake to begin to close that gap? Maybe she can offer to join a cross functional team that works with the various business units to update the five-year forecast. Perhaps she can take a continuing education class in business model development and long-range forecasting.

Fairly early in my marketing career, I bought one of those black-and-white composition books and listed the fifteen or twenty skills that I thought a really good marketer would have. I created the list by reading the leading books on marketing (especially Philip Kotler's book, *Marketing Management*) and by asking senior-level marketers, "What skills set apart really good marketers?" Then, I evaluated my current marketing capabilities against this list of skills. For example, at the age of thirty, I graded myself:

- "B+" in pricing tools and analysis;
- "B" in market segmentation, targeting, and product positioning;
- "A" in project/task force management;
- "D" in advertising agency management;
- "F" in trade marketing and selling; and
- "C" in new product development market research.

After completing this evaluation, I slowly but steadily figured out ways to narrow my skill gaps by lobbying to be placed on a new initiatives, seeking counsel from marketers known to be very competent in particular skill areas, and reading marketing books and trade articles. I would learn something and write it down in that composition book under the relevant skill heading. I still have that black book and pull it out and wave it around to my students at Kellogg (who snicker because the composition book is so "old school") to illustrate the importance of being deliberate and taking the initiative to develop a well-rounded "toolkit" and reduce skill gaps.

Seek Out Skill and Knowledge Expansion Opportunities

Work on improving your skills and broadening your experiential knowledge by participating in or leading a cross functional task force, volunteering for a non-job-related project, attending industry conferences, and signing up for developmental seminars and workshops. It's easy to dismiss these noncore activities amid the rush of your day-to-day job of delivering results and putting out fires. But you're robbing yourself of broadening opportunities. In particular, participating in or leading a task force has been cited as one of the most common developmental activities mentioned by successful executives. In my first task force experience, I participated, as the marketing representative, in the launch of a new line of salsas and dips at Frito-Lay. It was an eye-opening experience. For the first time in my seven-year tenure at PepsiCo, I saw how all the pieces of the puzzle fit together and interacted with each other. From sourcing the tomatoes and peppers to manufacturing the salsa to distributing the jars of salsa through the supply chain of regional and local distribution centers and onto the shelves of supercenters and convenience stores and then coordinating the sales and marketing activities to sell the products off the shelves, it was a tremendously broadening experience. That experience increased my understanding of Frito-Lay's value chain and "how to take a product to market."

Reduce Your "Business = Busy-ness" Quotient

Seeking out developmental opportunities means finding ways to reduce your "busy-ness" quotient. You must carve out the time to become strategic because it involves pursuing non-task-driven activities (such as attending an industry conference or interviewing a key supplier) that broaden your perspective and increase your understanding of the ecosystem in which you operate. Look for ways to:

- Prioritize your workload, finding ways to cut the number of low- or non-value-added tasks you do;
- Make sure you're not micromanaging and that you're delegating tasks appropriately; and
- Carve out time on a weekly basis to participate in at least one strategically broadening activity.

Read Up!

It's an obvious solution, but worth stressing, as nearly every successful person I've met reads extensively then synthesizes and applies what they've learned to their jobs. I would try to read:

- The major newspapers, such as the *Wall Street Journal* and *New York Times* (I peruse both to try to obtain a balanced perspective);
- Trade journals (for me, as a technology entrepreneur and venture capitalist, this would include publications like *Wired*, *TechCrunch*, and *VentureBeat*);
- Blogs (given my current line of work, this would include the blogs of thoughtful venture capitalists like Paul Graham, Fred Wilson, Bill Gurley, and Brad Feld, among others);

- Books (this endnote has a link to a website that lists the favorite books of business leaders and other influential people);
- Twitter (I recommend creating a well-curated list of people to follow—reading what they post is a great way to stay abreast of breaking news);
- News aggregators (current ones that are popular include Feedly, Pulse, and Google News); and
- Trend reports (such as Gartner Inc.'s trend report, J. Walter Thompson's "The Future 100 Trends to Watch" report, or technology analyst Mary Meeker's annual Internet trend report).

Get Out of the Office and Into the Field!

One of the best ways to broaden your perspective is to get out of the office and into the field, going on market tours where you look at competitors, visit with suppliers and buyers, and interview customers and consumers. Many of the most innovative ideas come from the field—from the salesforce, from the frontline troops, and so on. They're closest to the customer and see the market trends first.

One of the best ways to better understand your business is by spending time with the customer service team. Ask them about the customer issues that come up time and again. Ask them for three ways that the headquarters/management team could help them. Ask them for ideas they have for the business based on their dealings with customers.

When I was promoted to be the CEO of Walmart.com, I sought the counsel of a more experienced Walmart executive I admired. I asked him for words of wisdom, given my new assignment. He told me to make sure I "didn't get pinned into the corner office, taking endless meetings" and to instead block out time to get out into the field to see what's really going on. He told me to take control of my own work calendar and not farm it out for others to manage. He reminded me to talk to suppliers and customers, to tour stores with Walmart operators, and to evaluate competitors and learn from what they're doing. He said, "It's easy to lose touch with what's really going on, especially when you're in a consuming staff headquarters job."

Meet with External Consultants and Domain Area Experts

It's likely that there are many external experts who work and consult in your field, whether it's technical or general management consulting firms (such as Deloitte Consulting in financial services, Navigant in litigation and risk reduction, or McKinsey & Company in general business strategy) or other third-party agencies. Find a reputable firm that specializes in your area of interest and ask them about customer and technological trends in your industry. Ask them to take you through their process of examining a problem and then presenting it. How do they think through and structure a strategic presentation? When I was about thirty, after my boss questioned my "strategic orientation" in my performance review, I found a person from the Boston Consulting Group who had been doing consulting work with my company, Frito-Lay. I took her out for lunch and asked her how Boston Consulting Group examined new product development opportunities in the snack industry. She connected me to other consultants in her firm and I ended up seeking their counsel as well. I found the exchanges to be very useful in helping me examine and frame strategic opportunities for new product development in my industry.

Dabble; Become an Early Adopter of Something

Find new software tools or a new skill relevant to your job and become knowledgeable about it. Read up on it. Download it. Play with it. Break out of your comfort zone! I asked former CEO of Twitter Dick Costolo how he stays fresh and abreast of changes in the fast-moving world of technology. Although he's a voracious reader, he is also a dabbler. He said, "I try to use stuff as soon as it comes out. I play around with everything. I try to understand why a popular service or product is popular and why another one isn't. What can I learn from comparing the two? Whether it's virtual reality or new media, I get my hands on stuff and play." If you consider yourself a technological Luddite, try approaching your IT support team and asking them about new software tools and technologies they're evaluating or installing. Ask them to walk you through a few of them that are becoming more important. Because of what they do, I have found that the IT support staff love to talk tech. I bet I've sat down with IT support people fifty times and asked them about a new technology.

I think that if Gail, the high-performing controller at Warm Hearth, were to broaden her perspective by doing some of these exercises, she could move beyond her current level and attain a CFO position. The biggest question I have concerning Gail's situation is if she can reach the CFO position at her current company or if her progress will be impeded by her boss, Ron. It may be that Ron finds her to be a threat to his job, or it may be that Ron thinks Gail has reached her potential and isn't open to helping her build her future capabilities—in which case Gail may need to make a strategic move to another company to attain her goal of becoming a CFO.

CHAPTER 5

THE WHIRLING DERVISH

Overcommitting and Underdelivering

We've all worked with a Bill Smith, known to his peers, bosses, and subordinates as the Whirling Dervish. He's smart. He's original. He has fresh ideas for the business. But harnessing his talents is like grabbing a handful of wind.

As usual, Bill comes blowing into Speed Rez Corp.'s cross functional task force meeting late, apologizing and muttering about the traffic ("Are they ever going to get highway 28 straightened out?! Makes me crazy!"), beads of sweat accenting his forehead. Speed Rez is a customer service software company; the task force was set up by product manager Sally Jones to develop a recommendation to overhaul one of their legacy products—a helpdesk software solution. Eyes roll as Bill takes off his jacket and settles in, and Sally, the meeting chair, is forced to backtrack to get him up to speed. She then asks Bill for a progress update on his assigned portion of the project. People on the task force wait impatiently as the Whirling Dervish rifles through his computer bag, trying to locate his project file folder. Several Post-It notes with handwritten scrawl on them spill out of his bag and flutter to the ground. A fruit and nut bar plops on the floor. "Ah, here it is," exclaims the Whirling Dervish as he pulls out a file folder and opens it. But, oops, all that's in it is last month's electricity bill. Eventually, after more digging around, Bill gives up, sighs, and apologizes about inadvertently leaving the folder with its half-completed report at home. When Sally asks for a verbal update, the Whirling Dervish says, "Well, it's been a tough week, folks. My other job priorities — essentially my core accountabilities — have necessitated that I give less attention than I'd like to our initiative. But overall, let's just say that I feel good about what I found when I dug into competitive best practices." When Sally presses Bill to explain what exactly he feels good about, the Whirling Dervish offers several excellent insights around competitive areas of vulnerability that might allow the team to improve their legacy helpdesk product. The problem is, his extemporaneous comments soaked up fifteen minutes of valuable task force time, and the group, now well behind schedule, is left to sift through his remarks and figure out how they apply to improving the current feature set of their existing software product.

Whirling Dervishes stir up trouble and can derail due to:

- Poor planning, organizational, and task management skills;
- Difficulty prioritizing work and focusing on the activities that drive enterprise value;
- Being "pleasers" who have difficulty saying "no" to requests; and
- Underestimating the time and effort required to complete tasks or projects.

Whirling Dervishes are littered throughout our companies, creating chaos. In fact, the odds are you're working with one right now. And boy, does he try your patience. You've managed to get your teamwork done amid a sea of your own competing priorities, so why can't he? Enough with the excuses, Bill, just get your work done!

The Whirling Dervish, to put it simply, does not deliver on promises. His word is not his bond. So he ends up losing his personal credibility and coworkers slowly but surely back away and avoid working with him.

When talking about leadership to a group of entrepreneurial founders at a technology conference in 2015, Jamie Dimon, chief executive officer and chairman of the board at JPMorgan Chase put it this way when he talked about leadership: "The tone gets set because you walk the walk and you do what you say you're going to do." If you say you're going to do something, do it.

Not Delivering on Promises: Questions to Consider

Whirling Dervishes are often talented people with a lot of great ideas—but they have difficulty delivering on promises. To determine whether you may be at risk of falling into the trap of being a Whirling Dervish, ask yourself the following questions:

- Have you repeatedly received feedback from your colleagues, boss, or customers that you're late delivering on commitments?
- How would you rate your project management skills? Do you have effective methods for planning, organizing, and managing your work?
- Do you have an effective method for managing your electronic correspondences? Do you tend to touch e-mails once or multiple times?

- To what extent are you in control of your work calendar? Does your day consist of wall-to-wall meetings, or do you have discretion over your schedule? Do you create breaks in the day to get your own work done?
- How would you rate your ability to delegate work among members of your team?
- How comfortable are you in saying no to requests from your work colleagues?
- Do you find that you get swept up in the excitement of a new idea or project, commit to a course of action, and later wish you had given it more consideration?
- Are you clear on your most important goals and objectives for the quarter and the year? Are you clear on the three things that you must accomplish today? This week?

A vice president of human resources, Gene, told me about Alpana, a marketing director for a medical device company that produced and sold orthopedic equipment, who, like Bill, suffered from the Whirling Dervish syndrome—though hers manifested differently than Bill's. Alpana was very affiliative and sensitive from an interpersonal standpoint. She was full of good ideas and "was all about love and cheers." But she didn't know how to temper her many ideas—a recent one being to create a peer-to-peer social network to reduce prospective patients' anxiety over the prospects of a total knee replacement. Feedback from her team and coworkers from a 360-degree review included comments like, "She overwhelms her staff" and "When we're giving her project updates, she starts many comments with this ominous line, 'Wouldn't it be cool if we . . . .'" Alpana's team was never quite clear if she was bringing forth a new idea for them to chew on or if she was changing their set of priorities. When I asked Gene how he'd helped Alpana, he said,

The entry point was to understand what motivated her—and it was having warm and caring relationships with others—and then to show how her style was hurting people—that regardless of her good intentions, her team was suffering as a result of her lack of focus. Her constant shift in focus frustrated her team and was beginning to erode their trust in her as a manager and department leader. When she saw the ways in which her style was damaging her relationships, it motivated her, because she was a very kind person who was motivated by affiliation. I worked with her in particular on two things: to create visible, agreed-upon priorities for her team and on her own personal productivity—structuring her day, improving her meeting productivity, etc. This was hard for her because she was naturally this creative, fluid, off-the-cuff person. We talked a lot about centering and recentering on the "NOW." What's relevant right now? What do we need to accomplish right now?

Did she improve? Gene said, "Yes, she did. The only way you get improvement is if the person is motivated and Alpana was motivated because she cared about her team and wanted to be a good manager and leader. So she took the work seriously and became a more effective manager."

Where They Go Wrong

There are five reasons people like the Whirling Dervish have difficulty delivering on promises and run into career trouble: poor planning and organizational skills; difficulty prioritizing their work and staying focused on the high-impact activities; not understanding work flow processes (and often underestimating the time it takes to complete job activities); being a pleaser (not being able to say "no" and taking on too much work); and suffering from grandiosity (becoming enamored with "big ideas" and not staying focused on completing the fundamental tasks for which they are accountable).

Poor Planning and Organizational Skills

People who don't follow through are often disorganized and not detail oriented, which leads them to make commitments they fail to keep. Mark Blecher, the senior vice president of digital gaming and corporate development at Hasbro, told me about Tom, a man who worked in his group at a previous company. Tom was plenty smart, but he wanted to only do the "fun, sexy, creative stuff" and not mundane things like taking notes in meetings or summarizing his observations and distributing them to the rest of the team after attending a trade show. In general, Tom wouldn't write anything down and, as a result, had poor follow-through skills. He not only lacked discipline, he felt that certain tasks weren't worthy of his time. Blecher said,

> I couldn't get him to embrace the importance of documentation: of ideas and observations, of follow-up tasks, of anything. He'd sit there in meetings and let everyone else do "administrative" work. He thought it was beneath him. I gave him a tough quarterly review, but it didn't get through to him. Then I gave him a tough annual review and he left the company. Since then, he's been at three companies in the last few years. He's still not getting it. Leaders don't only lead by setting direction and making tough decisions, they also lead by setting an example for others to follow. They don't view things like note-taking as "beneath them." If a hole needs to be dug, they pick up a shovel and dig.

Trouble Prioritizing Work and Maintaining Focus of Effort

Effective managers are able to differentiate high-impact work from busywork and prioritize their time accordingly. They use various tools and heuristics to prioritize, plan, and execute their work. They are able to distinguish and place a single-minded emphasis on completing the work that moves their key performance metrics. They are able to focus. An affliction from which ineffective managers suffer is what I call "working in response mode," allowing interruption after interruption to impede their progress on important projects by responding, like Pavlov's dogs, every time a text or e-mail message comes in over the transom. I was recently asked by a talented entrepreneur if I had any advice on how he could become more productive. Having observed him in several meetings, I asked him to estimate the number of times per hour he paused to check in with his smart phone. He said he had no idea. I told him that in the last meeting I'd had with him, on a topic that was important to him, he'd picked up his phone over ten times. He smiled—but it was a tight smile. I then asked where he placed his smart phone when working on an important task—like writing his board of directors a performance update or reviewing the progress report on an important initiative. He admitted, "Right next to me, where I can grab it if I need to." I asked if he had bid on a new house and was awaiting the seller's response. "No," he replied. I asked if he was waiting on a potential client's response to a recent new business pitch. "No, not at the moment," he said. I asked, "Then what would happen if, while you're working on an important priority, you turned off the ringer and charged the phone in a wall plug over there across the room? Would Rome burn to the ground?" He smiled and said, "Got it."

Not Understanding Work Flow Process

Managers who have trouble with execution often lack an understanding of the work flow process required inside their business unit or company. They tend to have a naive or inadequate under-standing of action steps, the functional and cross functional dependencies, and the necessary stakeholder approvals required to complete an initiative inside their company. They usually assume they can accomplish activities or projects in an unrealistic time frame. Clarice Shriver, a vice president of new product develop-ment for an educational publishing firm, said,

> People run into real career trouble if they can't navigate their work inside their organization—if they don't understand who to bring in to their projects and when to bring them in. Our marketing director is a case in point. While she has good marketing skills, she doesn't have a good understand-ing of how the work gets done inside these four walls, so my department, new product development, has to swoop in for just about every project she does, verifying informa-tion, giving design direction, editing copy and proofreading, in order to bail her out. If she took the time to understand how things worked, and if she put a process management system in place that had checks and balances, my depart-ment wouldn't have to dive in and save her. There was a big incident last week after she missed a deadline, so I think this issue will be resolved pretty soon. I doubt she'll be around much longer.

Being a Pleaser

People who have trouble delivering on promises are often pleasers who have difficulty saying "no" to requests for fear of disappointing their boss or coworkers. As a result, they overcommit and underde-liver. Pleasers also have a tendency to overpromise. In an effort to seek the esteem or approval of their superiors and/or coworkers or by getting carried away with their own enthusiasm for an idea, it's common for pleasers to lay out an unrealistic project timeline—one that assumes every component and every detail will proceed on plan and on time, which of course never happens—and to overestimate a project's likely results ("This will goose our sales by at least 50 percent!").

I suffer from being a pleaser and need to maintain my awareness of this weakness and resist giving in to it in situations that could hurt my ability to deliver on my core responsibilities. I don't always succeed either. Right now, I'm kicking myself for buckling under pressure and accepting a persistent request from a senior-level administrator at my business school to create and teach a new entrepreneurship class. In addition to writing this book, I already teach another class at Kellogg and also work as a venture capitalist. The additional work required to develop a new class has made the past six months quite uncomfortable. I should have drawn the line and said firmly, "I'm happy to create the class, but it would need to be next year, in June, after I've finished a few big projects I'm currently working on."

Grandiosity

People whose self-image is based on grandiosity are often curious, highly conceptual people who are spirited and full of big ideas. When this trait goes into overdrive, however, their strength can become their weakness. They become enamored with their game-changing, high-concept ideas and are distracted from following through on the mundane tasks or projects for which they are accountable. Because they carry great enthusiasm for their ideas, they usually are effective at selling them to their coworkers, so they have a tendency, like a tornado, to suck others into their spinning path. As a result, they can get an entire group offtrack.

I experienced grandiosity firsthand when I once worked alongside a man I'll call Bob. He was highly creative and brimming with enthusiasm over developing and testing new ideas. He would listen to senior executives knock around the viability of a nascent idea and when they turned to him, instead of saying, "Interesting—let me look into that and get back to you" or "That sounds very interesting, but to do it, we would likely have to shift resources away from project x," he'd invariably pipe up, "Yeah, I think we can do that!" Unfortunately, Bob would get swept along in the excitement of the new idea and wouldn't take into account the opportunity cost of shifting resources away from his team's core deliverables. He was also unrealistic about the expected results—he would overpromise and underdeliver so consistently that one of our executives created a "Bob Dilution Index" that lowered any performance forecast he provided. Although this dilution index seemed funny at first, over time Bob became known as an unreliable "Mad Professor" whose judgment was questionable, and his reputation steadily eroded. I watched as his team members migrated out of the department he led and I wasn't surprised when I eventually read an announcement saying he'd left "to pursue other opportunities."

I recently spoke with John, a thirty-one-year-old data analyst who holds a bachelor's degree in finance. He has worked for the past nine years in the technology industry, primarily in financial services. Although clearly an intelligent guy, John has been fired twice in the past five years. When we talked, he was forthcoming and clear about why. "I've always been pretty quick—in college I got good grades and could take a big class load because I can process material quickly. But I tend to get bored by routine and I like to multitask. I like to have lots of stuff going on all the time. But the flip side of this is this lack of focus and poor attention to detail, which is triggered in particular when things are going well.

I stop checking and rechecking my work. I become complacent and make stupid mistakes." When I asked him why he was fired, John said,

Which time?! The first time, I was working in data analytics and reporting for a financial technology company that uses software to provide financial services and I thought I had a great handle on my job. I was cruising along, pumping out a lot of reports but, not testing, not QA'ing [providing quality assurance] them before releasing them to our business teams—who relied on the reports to understand exactly how we were performing and also to make decisions on stuff like how much we should charge for various services. I was fired because I thought a particular team beat their business plan and I reported that, but I calculated their performance incorrectly and they actually didn't beat their plan. It became a very big deal because our company then missed our overall business plan and I was flat-out fired because of it.

When I asked John the role his boss played in his derailment area, John said, "I had a good boss. He'd warned me to slow down, to actually decrease my output and focus more on each report and to check and recheck my calculations. But I didn't listen to him, probably because I was proud of how much work I could crank out. And I got fired." Cringing internally, I asked John about the reason behind his second dismissal. John said, "I was working for a credit card company and I made another careless mistake. It was during tax season and I was trying to do too many things at once. I didn't maintain my focus and I sent one client's data to another client. That was a security breach and it cost me my job." When I asked John if he was currently employed, he said,

Yes, I'm a data analyst for an e-commerce company. I feel fortunate that I got the job, given my history. My boss knows all about my history—it came out during the interview process and on reference checks. But she still hired me because I'm good at financial analysis. However, I know now that producing nine great reports super-fast doesn't matter if the tenth one has a big fat error. I guard against that every single day. I remind myself how much it hurt when I lost those jobs—how humiliating it was. And because I'm married, with three small kids, people depend on me. That makes me very motivated to slow down, stop multitasking, and check and recheck my work. Now I QA everything to death.

How to Get Better at Delivering on Promises

Whirling Dervishes, more often than not talented and creative people, can overcome their challenges and focus their effort to deliver on promises by working on six areas: being crystal clear on their primary job accountabilities; better understanding the work flow processes inside their organization; being more deliberate in planning and organizing their work; looking for opportunities to reduce the number of meetings they attend; working on their ability to say "no" to nonessential work requests; and improving their delegation skills.

Be Crystal Clear on Your Job Accountabilities

Work with your boss to develop your overall goals and objectives and performance evaluation criteria. I prefer to set accountabilities every six months because business priorities frequently change. Make sure there is clarity on two sets of metrics: those for your overall job, the quarterly or annual performance metrics for which you're being held accountable, and your key projects and assignments—when they're due and the performance expectation.

I was surprised, when interviewing managers who derailed, by the number of cases where they simply did not understand the performance criteria on which they were being measured or the key projects they needed to accomplish to have been viewed as turning in a strong performance. You can't do your job well if you're unclear on the objectives on which you're being evaluated.

Learn the Work Flow Process in Your Organization

Nearly every job in every organization has a set of process steps, formal or informal, that move a project from inception to completion. Whirling Dervishes who don't deliver on promises often don't understand the steps in work flow process—their proper sequence, how long each will take to complete, and whom to include along the way. They then often miss deadlines or make glaring mistakes because they don't know the right questions to ask.

Find someone in your organization with good project management skills and ask how to expedite initiatives through the maze, particularly identifying the key gatekeepers who approve and control the flow of resources and determining the typical bottlenecks that impede the speed or completion of projects. There's a company's formal organizational structure and then there's the real one—where and how the work *really* gets done. Many times the most powerful people in the organization are buried deep in the bowels of the place and understand the company's shorthand. You've got to figure out who they are and how to enlist their support to solve your problems.

When I worked at Frito-Lay, there was a man in the marketing department named Dave Philips. I didn't even know what Dave's title was—probably something vague like "Director of Program

Management." Although he wasn't one of the senior officers in the department, he wielded a surprising amount of power and had deep knowledge of the inner workings of our company. He could give your project the green light, help you secure resources (both people and money), and get your budget approved, and he could connect you to the right people in various departments to expedite your project. Taking the time to explain your initiative to Dave Philips and gaining his support was like receiving Willy Wonka's golden ticket. Once, merely days after I'd taken over the salsa and dips business (and didn't really know what the hell I was doing), I was reviewing internal and retail sales data and saw that massive quantities of our new "zesty" cheese dip, which was aimed to compete against Kraft's Cheez Whiz, was going stale. The jars were past the "best consumed by" code date and were being pulled from supermarket shelves. I had established a good working relationship with Dave, so one day he was kind enough to come by my office and say, "Let me show you something." He took me through me an internal report (which I didn't even know existed) that showed an alarming number of cases of our new zesty cheese dip that were clogged inside our internal distribution network, in various regional and local distribution centers all over the United States. He said, "The problem may not be in the supermarket; the problem may be right here in our own supply chain." Then, seeing my confused look, he said, "Sit down. Let's call some of the supply chain directors in the field offices and see what they think." We made a handful of calls and found that our sales force had ordered such a large supply of the new product that it was backing up inside our own distribution network. By the time the cheese dip had reached grocery stores and supermarkets, it had a short shelf life left. No wonder it was going stale on retail shelves. In this case, one of the key work flow steps was realizing the importance of working with the Frito-Lay supply chain managers (who take the field's sales orders and allocate them throughout various distribution centers in the United States) and comparing their regional distribution center orders with my own regional retail sales forecasts to make sure they are similar. In this case, they weren't.

Be Deliberate in Planning and Prioritizing Your Work

Be thoughtful and intentional about planning and prioritizing your work before automatically diving in and executing it. You know the old adage: "Plan the work; then work the plan." Here are four tips that could help Bill Smith, the Whirling Dervish who had so much trouble organizing and planning at the beginning of the chapter.

First, take a look at David Allen's *Getting Things Done*, or his follow-up book, *Making It All Work*. These books have very useful frameworks about mastering work flow.

Second, try to approach your day in segments, setting aside sacred time when you're most productive to conduct strenuous intellectual work. To the extent possible, e-mail and respond to others during nonproductive time and do so in batches. Don't respond to texts and e-mails as they flow into your in-box since that puts you in response mode, allowing the tail to wag the dog. I try to adhere to the following plan:

- I set aside 6:00–8:00 a.m. for "thinking work" where I read, write, or work on a thorny problem;
- From 8:00 to 9:00 a.m. I go through my e-mail in-box, reading and responding to others;
- From 9:00 a.m. to noon I block out time to have conversations and attend meetings;

- From noon to 1:30 p.m. I often schedule lunches with customers, suppliers, and other key constituents and work associates;
- From 1:30 to 2:00 p.m. I try to block out time to again go through my e-mail in-box and respond to any urgent requests;
- From 2:00 to 4:00 p.m. I set aside time for more conversations and meetings; and
- From 4:00 to 5:00 p.m. I respond to any pressing issues and plan my work for the following day.

Although I realize you can't always schedule your day or week the way you'd like, it's still a good practice to try to structure and manage it and not let it manage you. Generally, I've found people have more discretion over their schedules than they think they do.

Third, take the time, on a regular basis, to look at all the things on your plate and look for opportunities to prune! Ask yourself, "Of this laundry list of activities, which really move the needle? Which are my most time-consuming activities that add little value?" Personally, I follow a simple A-B-C method, placing my various work activities into three buckets: The A's are time-sensitive must-do critical activities. B's are capability-building activities, such as spending time in the field, that help improve my performance as well as my team's. And the C's consist of the daily slog-through category—the somewhat-important, somewhat-urgent stuff— filling out reports, responding to e-mails—that eventually needs to get done.

Fourth, consider using simple software planning tools to increase your productivity. Whether it's using a planning template like the Gantt chart, a software planning tool like Base Camp or Asana, or a communication management tool like Evernote or Microsoft OneNote, take the time to explore various solutions to help manage your workload. If this seems like a foreign language and you're bewildered, ask a good project manager for help or Google "personal productivity tools" and explore options.

Learn How to Say No

If some of the balls you're juggling are starting to drop and you feel like you're becoming a Whirling Dervish, you may have trouble saying "no" when people request your time. This is certainly the case with me. I need to frequently remind myself that when I say "no" to someone's request, I'm saying "yes" to something else that is important to me, whether it's a key work project for which I'm accountable or to free up my time to see my daughter's soccer game or get in a gym workout.

Second, learn how to turn a request into a five-minute favor. For example, although you may not be able to take the time to speak at an event, you can take a few minutes to suggest a few speakers who are knowledgeable on that topic. And guard against the common tendency of getting swept up in the excitement of an idea and then committing prematurely to a course of action. I'm a card-carrying offender in this area, too. I remind myself time and again to hit the pause button before committing to something about which I'm enthusiastic. I've gotten better—by learning to pause and buy myself time to reflect and reconsider before agreeing to a course of action.

I recently had breakfast with an entrepreneur who had just sold his business to another company. It wasn't a profitable exit for him—it was an "acqui-hire" where his company was bought for the skills and expertise of his team rather than for the value of the company's products and services. When I asked him key lessons learned from his time launching and running the start-up, he said, "I realize in hindsight that I got caught up in an endless stream of requests—to be on start-up panels, to mentor students and other start-up founders, to tell our start-up's story to noncore constituents and so forth. I spent way too much time on that stuff and not enough time on the nitty-gritty aspects of building the business." The bottom line of learning to say "no" is this: it's your life, not the requestor's. If you don't show discretion over the allocation of your precious time, who will?

Improve Your Delegation Skills

Delegating, when done well, not only frees up your time to focus on key priorities, it also motivates others and helps develop their skills. Delegating also reduces the number of organizational "choke points" and moves activities off the plates of overloaded managers.

*

Strong performers are good at managing their most precious resource—their own time—and show the discipline of identifying and prioritizing the activities most important to their jobs and company's success. By doing so on an ongoing basis they stay focused on what matters. When Bill Smith—a.k.a. the Whirling Dervish—feels unfocused and overwhelmed by the list of tasks in front of him, he needs to ask himself, "Which of these activities are paramount to achieving the goals and objectives I've set with my boss? Which of my activities improves the customer experience and deepens their engagement with our company?" At the end of the day, that's the ultimate barometer of where he should be spending his time.

The thread that connects the Whirling Dervish with Captain Fantastic, the Solo Flier, Version 1.0, and the One-Trick Pony is their need for self-reflection to better understand the vulnerabilities that could impede their career progression.

Among the over one hundred people I examined who derailed, those who emerged stronger from the event took the following path: They first sought and found emotional support from family, friends, and professional career coaches and counselors. With the help of others, they were able to reframe the derailment event, choosing to view it as a learning experience that would make them wiser and improve their performance over time. Second, they maintained a sense of agency, taking responsibility for their actions and their recovery, by addressing the issue head-on by determining where they were weak and seeking additional training to address behavioral issues or fill skill gaps. In some cases, they made career changes, aligning themselves with jobs for which they had greater interest or passion.

In the final analysis, people who recovered took accountability for their derailment event by being reflective about the role they played in getting fired or demoted. And then they were deliberate in determining what they needed to do to ensure it didn't happen again. One person I interviewed who recovered from a derailment event and was later promoted showed the accountability that was typical for those who got back on track, saying, "After being fired, I realized that 90 percent of what happens to you is directly related to your own choices and actions. You better understand them." Another told me, "I took advantage of it [being fired] and made it an opportunity to learn about myself and then reset my career." A third said, "Derailing made me better—stronger. I learned about myself from the whole debacle."

The first and most important learning for those who recovered concerned themselves—self-reflection, leading to self-understanding, became the key that unlocked the door to their recovery.

PART TWO

ACCELERATING YOUR CAREER

CHAPTER 6

THE RIGHT STUFF

hy do some careers flourish while others stall? That was the key question I posed on the very first page. Does it come down to smarts? Is innate IQ the distinguishing characteristic of people with "the right stuff"? Interestingly, it isn't. Certainly, IQ plays a part in determining the likelihood of a person reaching a high-level position of leadership, in particular one's ability to process a lot of information, spin future scenarios of possible outcomes, and make sound decisions. But IQ is not as much of a predictor of future success as you might imagine. A host of studies indicate that IQ only accounts for about 25 percent of the variance in job success. In other words, three-fourths of performance is accounted for by factors besides that of raw intelligence.

So what other factors *really* matter? Are there competencies or behaviors we can develop to help accelerate career success? In a nutshell, yes, and that is our focus in this second part.

A Profile of the Right Stuff

Dan Marriott, who methodically worked his way up from modest means to creating his own successful private equity investment firm, is a compelling example of someone who embodies the right stuff principles.

Dan grew up on a hog farm in central Illinois and went on to receive his bachelor's degree in agricultural economics and finance and then his MBA from the University of Illinois. He then landed a job in the purchasing department at Frito-Lay, where he bought raw materials like corn, wheat, and soybeans. After a few years in purchasing, Dan, realizing that he was in a support function and that the marketers and sellers were on the "critical path" and drove the agenda at Frito-Lay, managed to transfer into the marketing department. He secured that position at the ripe old age of twenty-five by leading the launch of a new salsa product after the marketing manager in charge of the effort suddenly left the company. Dan, representing the purchasing department in the product launch task force, took over the reins when none of the more senior members assumed the responsibility for the launch. So Dan stepped into the leadership vacuum, took charge, and led the task force, keeping the launch on track for several months until a new product marketing manager was brought in to take over. That new marketer was me.

In the first month on the job, while I became acquainted with the industry, met various constituents, and tried to determine the key business deliverables for my new assignment, I kept Dan on the task force to provide continuity and watched him in action. Even though he was young, he led the task force with ease. He was knowledgeable from an operational perspective, understanding the company's supply chain and the steps required to bring the new salsa through our distribution system and to our retail markets, and he was well organized and ran the task force meetings efficiently. I noted the extent to which he had the respect of the older, more experienced task force members. So the first official action I took in my new job? I hired Dan Marriott.

Over the next few years, armed with his operational knowledge of Frito-Lay's manufacturing and supply chain process, an inquisitive nature, and an incredible work ethic, Dan rose up through the brand management ranks, developing his functional marketing skills and receiving three promotions in five years. He eventually left Frito-Lay, lured by opportunities in the dynamic, fast-paced Internet economy. He committed himself to understanding the fundamentals of Internet software development and user experience in the new digital media landscape (avoiding the Version 1.0 trap) and went on to become the chief marketing officer and then later the president of online city guide Citysearch, a division of media and Internet company InterActiveCorp (IAC).

During his time at IAC, Dan continued to broaden his skill set by working in finance and business strategy. He made a lateral move into strategic planning and later became the executive vice president of corporate strategy and business development, working directly with IAC's founder, billionaire Barry Diller. By taking these developmental assignments into functions like finance, strategy, and business development, Dan prepared for the job he'd always wanted: being an entrepreneur and launching his own private equity firm.

Dan is currently a managing partner of Stripes Group, a growth equity firm he cofounded in 2008 that has invested in successful early-stage companies like SmartWool, GoFundMe, and Blue Apron. When I asked Dan about his journey from his modest means to accomplishing all he had in the business world, he reinforced the importance of being curious and taking charge of your own career, saying,

> As I rolled into college straight off the farm, I came to a few realizations fairly quickly. First, I didn't know much of anything about anything and didn't know anyone. I ate sushi

for the first time in my twenties. I felt like the world was an inside joke to my peers, and I had to figure out the punch line. Second, I realized that I was smart enough to succeed. Third, I realized that the one variable that I could control— and that was in my genes—was work ethic. If I kept my eyes open for opportunities to add value, worked three times harder than anyone else, and treated everyone around me really well, I would win most days. Not all days, but most. I didn't see that same level of commitment in my peers—and I was energized by that fact. The people around me seemed to do what they were told but didn't look to add value beyond the specific tasks they were given. It became a bit of a secret to me. I knew I could find areas to add value beyond the let- ter of my job. Sure, the light in my office would be on much later than anyone else's—that was OK. My motivation sim- ply came from having no alternatives in life—no way back. While I loved growing up on a farm, and all that came with it, that was no place for me. It was a tough life and on the wrong side of too many economic headwinds. Each profes- sional step since I left the farm has been built on a simple approach—find areas I could add real value and make sure I am associating with smart, fun people of real integrity who do things the right way. Then show up early with a hot cup of coffee and do all I can to hit the nail on the head harder than anyone they have ever seen. And always be grateful for the opportunity and remember that the people around me play a much bigger role in my own success than I do in theirs.

When Dan spoke of taking the initiative, of "looking for oppor- tunities to add real value," he stressed the importance of having a learner's mind-set, which is a key theme throughout this book. Although I worked with Dan twenty years ago, one of his traits still

fresh in my memory is his curiosity. Dan asked more questions —
and good questions — than anyone I've ever worked with. In meetings, instead of telling people what he thought, he asked people
what they thought. He said,

> I try to maintain a high level of intellectual curiosity about
> everything and everyone. Meet lots of people with divergent
> views who do interesting things — ask questions, listen well,
> and soak it all up. Read absolutely anything I can get my
> hands on. Who knows? The back two pages of a research
> report read on a long plane flight (instead of taking a nap)
> might illuminate another thought I've had and connect two
> dots to a third idea — an idea that others in my industry might
> not see so clearly. Stay awake, keep moving, ask lots of ques-
> tions others may be afraid to ask — and process it all quickly.
> Do it day in and day out. If I combine this with honed pat-
> tern recognition from my various career experiences, I'll be
> able to play a pretty good hand in life.

Components of the Right Stuff

People who have the right stuff, like Dan Marriott, aren't great at
everything — no one is (with one possible exception, baseball Hall
of Famer Willie Mays, who could hit, field, and run equally well,
arguably better than anyone in each position). But they are good
at a handful of things that matter. Success is not a matter of perfection, of mastering all the competencies — the skills and behaviors
needed to perform well in a job — that are laid out by an organization. People with the right stuff, those who rise up to leadership positions in their businesses, are in the top quartile of their company in
no more than three to five of the ten to twelve competencies that
their organizations track and use for performance development

and management. *But they focus their attention on becoming excellent at the right ones.*

To determine if you're focusing on developing the right strengths, ask yourself these two questions:

- *Do I have the right strengths in my current position, relative to people doing similar work?* In my own case, at Frito-Lay, I focused in particular on developing strong trade marketing relationships with our field sales force and the retail grocery buyers in order to get my chip and dip products into retail distribution and into the hands of the consumer. Although this was a critically important competency at Frito-Lay, I noticed that many of my marketing peers didn't take the time to fly out to our regional sales offices and to the retail grocer's headquarters on a weekly basis in order to develop these relationships.
- *Do I have the right strengths around which to build my career in order to succeed in the future?* In Dan Marriott's case, he wisely broadened his skill set and became skilled in technology marketing and business development and later in finance, which allowed him to fulfill his dream of launching his own private equity investment company. Dan, with his willingness to take smart career risks in order to develop his acumen in functional areas that would become useful at a later date, is the antithesis of Version 1.0 (who lacks adaptability) and the One-Trick Pony (who has a narrow band of skills and hits a premature career ceiling).

To answer the first question, you must know how your strengths stack up in the competency areas that *really* matter in your position. And you need to know this relative to others who are doing the same type of work and competing for the same job positions. For example, if you're a technical product manager it would be critical to have very strong organizational skills as well as the ability to communicate effectively with other departments with which you'll be working. Are you more competent at those critical things than your fellow product managers with whom you're competing for jobs? If you're a vice president at a venture capital firm, are you better at networking—at combing the market and finding great new deals—than your peers at other venture capital firms? If you're a software enterprise sales manager, do you have better selling skills, in order to close new customers, than your competitors at other companies?

Dan Marriott excelled at thinking outside the box. He was very curious, asked probing questions, and was able to find new avenues of business growth. He also had strong analytical skills, so he could evaluate his product portfolio's pricing strategy and make adjustments to improve overall profitability, or he could evaluate the effectiveness of his advertising spend and make adjustments to improve his return on investment. Both of these areas—thinking outside the box and having strong analytical skills—are crucial competencies for product marketing managers.

So make sure you know the job competencies that *really matter*. Ask your boss or talented people who've been in your shoes and have been promoted in a job like yours. Find out how you stack up in these competency areas relative to your peer group. Then you'll know the areas on which to focus your professional skill development. In my case, I asked Paul Davis, who'd risen through the marketing and sales ranks and into a general management position at PepsiCo (and later became the CEO of Kettle Chips, and after that, Coinstar), what marketing skills were important to develop. Paul told me two things. First, develop strong relations with R&D in order to secure the resources required to develop new product extensions, because a steady stream of product news to retail customers is one of the key drivers of incremental revenue at Frito-Lay. And second, to make sure I was well-aligned with our sales force, in order to have their support and attention. Paul told me that while we had three hundred active items at Frito-Lay, the sales force could only focus on selling about one hundred of them into retail accounts. "You must make sure they're behind you, so your product is one of those one hundred!"

Second, you want to work on developing the right strengths— ones that will allow you to succeed in the future. Research shows that people with the right stuff exhibit three strengths in particular that allow them to succeed in increasingly challenging assignments:

- They act on their own *initiative*—they are learners who pursue a variety of self-starting methods to foster their continued professional and personal development and they seek out challenging assignments that will accelerate their skill development and allow them to realize career advancement opportunities. Dan Marriott is a perfect example of this. He sought broadening assignments and after developing his skill set in marketing, moved into strategic planning and finance, which provided him with tremendous career flexibility.
- They have emotional intelligence, which allows them to *build positive relationships with others.* In doing so, they avoid the interpersonal problems of a Captain Fantastic.
- And third, they have tremendous perseverance and *drive for results.* They establish stretch goals, focus on the work that provides the greatest return on investment, and take personal responsibility for the outcomes of the group. In

doing so, they avoid becoming an unfocused Whirling Dervish.

In terms of all the competencies organizations use for employee skill development, having these three surpasses all others in gauging the likelihood of a person becoming a top performer over time.

Of these three strengths, none is more important than *taking the initiative.* High performers with the right stuff accelerate their personal and professional development by having a "learning orientation"—a curiosity to constantly learn and improve. This disposition allows them to derive meaning out of experiences so they learn from the past and don't repeat their mistakes. They have the ability to determine what to do when they're stuck. They are curious and seek out new knowledge and experiences. They read a lot, from industry news and white papers to "how-to" books and biographies. They have a passion for inquiry, asking, "How might we . . ." and "If we tried this, what would happen?" They ask questions to understand how things work today, why the current state is what it is, and how it might be improved. They seek feedback on their own performance—they want to hear the constructive criticism of others in order to improve. They view conversations as opportunities to learn from others' experiences.

Stanford psychologist Carol Dweck calls this learning orientation "having a growth mindset." Dweck found, from her extensive research, particularly with students, that those who believed their intelligence could be developed (a growth mind-set) outperformed those who believed their intelligence was static (a fixed mind-set). Their primary goal wasn't to win or get an "A" but to grow, to improve, to get better at their activity. People who have a growth mind-set know that succeeding is an output of their focus on constant improvement. Often people derail because they fail to learn new skills and develop new capabilities. With constantly changing circumstances driven by technological advances, workers must rapidly learn and develop new skills. Derailed managers and executives often suffer from a lethal combination of overconfidence and narrow-mindedness. They experience success, it goes to their head, and they "know it all" and stop listening and soliciting input. They then rely on what worked in the past and become victims of their own success. They end up losing the very learning agility that allowed them to rise through the organization in the first place! Eddy—Version 1.0 from Chapter 3—comes to mind. Although he had become a successful sales manager, his lack of interest in understanding his company's technical product capabilities versus that of his competitors reduced his ability to land new business.

Regarding the second key strength, *"building positive relationships with others,"* people with the right stuff see themselves as leaders (whether they oversee a big team or are in a role as an individual contributor) who, regardless of their title, have the ability to create positive change in their organization. They adopt a positive attitude about their work, even when the business environment is tough. They know that energy and enthusiasm is contagious. (I have a saying: "Anyone can say what's wrong. Be the one who says what's possible.") These high performers are able to build strong relationships and enlist the support of others because of their strong emotional intelligence. According to a decade's worth of 360-degree feedback data collected on business managers and leaders, issues related to having low EQ, "emotional intelligence"—being defensive, insensitive, arrogant, volatile, and lacking empathy for others—accounts for over 50 percent of the reasons for career derailment. The competencies rated the weakest by managers and leaders in the same ten-year study included "patience," "listens well," "understands others," and "manages conflict effectively." The EQ skills that people with the right stuff have can be broken down into self-reflection, self-awareness, self-regulation, and social understanding.

Self-reflection, self-awareness, and self-regulation are intrapersonal competencies occurring inside a person's mind. They involve all our internal thought processes: sensing, perceiving, interpreting, and evaluating events. It's the ability to understand and then control our emotions, to stay calm under pressure and manage wayward impulses and desires. As Lao Tzu said over two thousand years ago, "Managing others is strength. Managing yourself is power."

"High-performing managers," says Harry Kraemer, the former CEO of Baxter, a multi-billion-dollar health care company, "take the time to figure out what matters to them in terms of values, purpose, and direction. People who derail lack the quality of self-reflection. They don't plan well and are constantly surprised. 'I'm surprised there was a fire in the plant!' (You're mixing chemicals in there—you should have contingency plans in anticipation of these events.) 'I'm surprised that my wife left me!' (You're traveling five days a week.) 'My two boys ignore me!' (You don't spend any time with them.)"

Kraemer then paused and said, "By being self-reflective, you can anticipate and problem-solve. Successful people avoid derailing because even when things are going well, they know things will change. On the opposite end of the spectrum you have derailed managers, who think, 'That wasn't fair!' These people think things shouldn't happen to them. But 'fair' and 'unfair' happen to everyone, all the time. You have to plan for them.

"Having high self-awareness allows us to be cognizant of, and then manage around, our own derailment propensities. By knowing what they're good at and bad at, self-aware people are less likely to find themselves in situations that play to their weaknesses. And if they do, knowledge of their areas of vulnerability allows them to develop compensatory strategies."

The final EQ skill, social understanding, is the genuine desire to understand not only another person's specific argument but also its subtext—the underlying reason for their perspective. People with the right stuff seek to have a holistic understanding of other people—taking into account their background, their needs, and their aspirations. They listen carefully, are empathetic, and try to put themselves in the other person's position. Given this orientation, they have a flexible leadership style, using different managerial and communication approaches, depending on the situation, to be effective and persuasive with others.

Greg Welch, a senior partner at executive search firm Spencer Stuart, values the wisdom the folk idiom embodies in the saying that "God gave you two ears and one mouth—use them in that ratio." Really strong performers, Welch believes, have strong social intelligence. They know when to listen and absorb; they know when to speak up and contribute. "A lot of people fill the airwaves. Star performers offer up rich nuggets that move the conversation forward." Greg's comment reminded me of a saying: "Seek first to understand, then to be understood."

Brock Leach, the former CEO of Tropicana, said,

> Overall, I think there are two long-term career differentiators. The first one is knowing yourself—your strengths, weaknesses, and the areas where you could be vulnerable. Where are your workarounds—the areas where you're not so strong and need other people to help you? The second is having emotional intelligence. It's your ability to understand others as well as being able to read how others respond to you. Without having strong EQ, your career is capped—period. Even if you're super smart and work hard, you'll get

offtrack without it. I see it all the time. People get so bought
in to their own cause that they get tunnel vision and can't see
the other person's point of view.

Here are a few questions to ask yourself as you think about
building positive relationships with others:

- Do you look for ways to foster strong team morale?
- When working with other departments, do you look for
  opportunities to add value beyond your job description
  and bridge the gap between departments—taking on tasks
  in those areas where no one seems willing to take the lead?
- Do you ask how you can help others achieve their goals
  and objectives?
- Are you empathetic and compassionate toward others—do
  you ask your coworkers how they're doing and where you
  can be of service to them?
- Do you share information and resources and assist others
  in meeting their critical business needs?
- Are you open-minded? Do you respect diversity of thinking, valuing differences in style and perspectives?
- Do you listen carefully and avoid dominating the
  conversation?

Laura Flanagan, the CEO of Foster Farms, talked about the
humility of high-potential performers on her team and their ability to work well with others. "The high-potential managers I work
with have the ability to engage others as coauthors. They don't
need to take all the credit for the end result. Others want to work
with them. What separates the good from the great managers is
their ability to lead, and that starts with having good interpersonal
skills."

Ruth Malloy, a consultant for executive search firm Spencer Stuart's Leadership Advisory Services, studied the traits and behaviors of high-potential performers. Very consistent with the above findings, Ruth told me that two strengths of high performers were their ability to "take the initiative" and to "work well within teams." "Most organizations identify high potentials by their initiative but miss the latter," she said. "High-potential managers scan their environment; they take the time to go deep and understand the players and how things fit together in the projects they're on. They determine what really matters and where the gaps are in being able to get those things done. Then they can place themselves in positions where they can add the most value, where they can be the most helpful. This creates a lot of goodwill and, as a nice side effect, builds their network along the way. They also build goodwill by listening well. High-potential people have a genuine interest in others' perspectives."

The *Tao Te Ching* is a book I recommend to my students at the Kellogg School of Management. An ancient text of Chinese wisdom, it has many passages that point to the power of leading through humility and service. One of my favorites:

> *A leader is best*
> *When people barely know he exists*
> *Of a good leader, who talks little,*
> *When his work is done, his aim fulfilled,*
> *They will say, "We did this ourselves."*

Lao Tzu, the author of *Tao Te Ching*, also said, "If you don't assume importance, you can never lose it." Instead of trying to control people, Lao Tzu advises us to trust people and gently guide them from behind the scenes, leaving no trace. Ultimately, there's a great satisfaction knowing that the example we're setting helps others make the right choices.

Regarding the third and final key strength, *"driving for results,"* people with the right stuff are achievement oriented and want to work in environments where performance is measured so they will know how they're doing. They seek to understand the standard of excellence for their assignment and try to place themselves in positions where they'll be held accountable for results.

People with the right stuff respond well when things don't go as planned. They lead with a cool head under stressful circumstances. They have the emotional resilience and grit to bounce back from failure, seeing it as a learning experience, not a personal indictment.

High performers are driven by completion of the work itself. More than money or status, they cite their ability to complete the work, to contribute and make a tangible difference as their primary motivator. Their intrinsic motivation to make a difference gives them the wherewithal to fight for difficult goals and persevere through adversity.

So ask yourself: Do you set challenging goals and make sure they're measurable? Do you track your progress against them on an ongoing basis? Do you have a high bias for action—a sense of urgency to get things done? Do you have tenacity and willpower—an attitude that no matter what, even if you have to work late and on weekends, you'll get your project over the goal line before time expires on the clock?

Doug Kush, a partner at global leadership advisory firm Egon Zehnder, stressed that drive is a critical trait of people with high potential. "When recruiting for firms," Kush said, "one of the most important things we're looking for is evidence that candidates have a 'do what it takes' attitude. Reaching a senior-level position

The Right Stuff Framework

requires endurance and the wherewithal to continue when others are tired. It requires a willingness to sacrifice. Does the candidate have that drive to succeed?"

The Right Stuff: A Framework

Drawing from leadership research as well as my own experience with high performers at PepsiCo, Walmart, Electronic Arts, and a variety of start-ups I've helped to launch and manage, I developed a framework that encapsulates five key components of having the right stuff:

- The *job skills* to succeed in your functional area, such as marketing, sales, supply chain operations.
- A deep understanding of an *industry*: the political, socio-economic, and technological factors affecting it as well as the power dynamics in its ecosystem, including the power of buyers, sellers, suppliers, and competitors.
- The *operational ability* to prioritize work and the knowledge of how to get things done within the infrastructure of your organization.
- *Distinctive strengths*: the three critical behavioral components just covered—taking the initiative, having the ability to build positive relationships, and having a strong drive for results.
- *Derailers*: the five job stallers and stoppers I have discussed throughout the book. If left unattended, they act

as massive divisors in the equation and cut away at your strengths and competencies and thus impede your career progress.

Job Skills: Knowing What to Do

The price of entry to the senior leadership circle is a strong set of skills in your chosen area or field of specialization, whether in the business realm (in areas like finance, operations, human resources, marketing, sales software application development) or any other trade or profession. People with the right stuff, particularly in the early part of their careers, focus their attention on developing specific job skills enabling them to solve problems. A set of strong functional skills becomes career capital—a key point of leverage when negotiating for a higher salary or looking for a new job. It drives their market demand. They know, however, that they need adequate time to fully develop these job skills. My experience is that it takes a sustained effort for at least six to eight years to develop a deep and well-rounded set of functional job skills. Here's why: If there are approximately ten primary skill areas in a functional job category like brand marketing, enterprise sales, supply chain logistics, or corporate finance, to become a functional expert, you'll probably need to have deep knowledge of four or five job areas and a good working knowledge of four or five others. If you work diligently on a particular job assignment for three or four years you will become skilled in three job areas. Then if you're moved into a different role (within the same function) you will work to develop skills in three more areas. So, generally, it takes several job rotations in this six-to-eight-year period—or at least having a variety of job assignments inside the same job position—to develop a deep and well-rounded skill set in a particular functional area.

For example, I worked in consumer marketing for a full decade before I felt confident enough to take my proverbial toolkit into the wild world of early-stage technology start-ups. In those years, I had five different marketing jobs within various divisions of PepsiCo:

- A restaurant marketing communications job at Pizza Hut Canada where I was part of a team that launched Pizza Hut Delivery into all Canadian provinces;
- A channel development job at Frito-Lay where I was part of a team responsible for expanding Frito-Lay's presence in convenience stores throughout the United States;
- A trade sales and marketing job in the western United States where I sold Frito-Lay marketing programs into food retailers like Safeway and Costco;
- A new product marketing job where I was part of the team that developed Tostitos Scoops; and
- A brand management job where I was a brand marketing director responsible for increasing revenue for Frito-Lay's corn products and salsa and dips.

In each assignment, I developed and honed a particular set of skills in the overall product marketing repertoire. For example, in my new product position at Frito-Lay, I learned how to conduct primary market research and segment, position, and launch new products into test markets. In my Tostitos brand management job, I learned how to evaluate and adjust pricing and develop strong advertising campaigns to drive consumer demand. In my trade sales and marketing job, I learned how to sell for space inside a retail environment. By the time I left my consumer goods marketing career at Frito-Lay to move into early-stage tech start-ups, I had developed a set of transferrable marketing skills that would serve me well in many different business environments, whether I was marketing game software products (Electronic Arts) or developing a new business that would sell diamonds to men (Blue Nile).

It's hard for people to develop this broad and deep skill set in a functional arca if they aren't patient with their careers, placing the priority on building functional skills over time versus getting itchy and job-hopping for the quick promotion. Here's a very common scenario I've encountered. In this case, I'm the vice president of marketing at Electronic Arts and I'm interviewing Mike, who is pursuing the position of director of marketing for our *EA Sports* franchise.

Mike and I are on opposite sides of a table and I'm looking over his résumé. It's a maze of stops, starts, and shifts. First he had a twelve-month stint as a product quality assurance tester at a game software company; then he had eighteen months as an associate marketing manager for a movie studio in Hollywood. That was followed by two years as an event marketing manager for a video game publisher. Finally Mike had eighteen months as a director of business development for a midsized e-commerce sporting goods retailer.

I can't find any rhythm to his résumé and I don't see his sweet spot. So I ask Mike two questions: "First, would you please tell me three things you're *really* good at in marketing? And second, for each thing you're good at, would you please give me an example of how you used that skill to make a meaningful improvement in your organization's performance?"

Because Mike's job-hopping into various industries didn't enable him to develop a cohesive set of job skills in the marketing function, the chances are fairly high that he won't be able to provide a credible answer to the first question and the chances are even higher that he won't be able to answer the second question well either. What meaningful changes could he have achieved in his twelve-to-eighteen-month stints at various companies? When you go into a new organization, it takes you the first year to find the bathroom and figure out how the coffee machine works. (And once you figure out how to make a nice big cup of coffee, you damn well should make sure you know where the bathroom is.) It takes time to become acclimated to a new environment and to determine how things are done. In the second year you know enough to build a plan and begin to execute it. And then, in year three, you see how your plan worked and you change or modify it. So my rule of thumb is you need to be at a place at least three years to make a real difference and have some meaty proof points as to your business acumen. So unless you're in a start-up—where time, given its frantic pace, is often measured in dog years—it is unlikely that you can create meaningful change in eighteen months.

I sometimes describe it like this to the students at the Kellogg School of Management: "Think of yourself as a really good mechanic. An organization hires you to come in with your jingling belt of tools, assess the situation, take out the right instrument, and fix the problem. They pay you based on your ability to have the tools and the skills to fix the problem. Later down the road, with experience, you can move from a mechanic to a designer. But your first goal is to take the time to become a really good mechanic who solves problems. That's why you're hired—it's your calling card, the career capital you have to offer."

When I was the CEO of Walmart.com, I set aside Friday afternoons for open office hours and encouraged anyone in the company, regardless of level and position, to come in and chat with me about anything—a new idea, a problem they're facing, anything at all. I recall having very talented people come into my office and talk about their desire to be promoted—sometimes they'd want this promotion within nine or twelve months of starting a new job—without having developed the requisite functional skill set or having put any points on the board. I would listen patiently while they attempted to make their case, but in the end my message was almost always this: "Please be patient and concentrate on building skills in your area of expertise and creating meaningful business impact. Regardless of potential, actual promotions follow competency and performance."

Industry Knowledge—Knowing Why to Do It

Although it's critically important to have a set of strong functional skills, it's not enough. People with the right stuff are very deliberate in choosing an industry in which to specialize and they take the time to develop a strong understanding of that industry. They are curious and externally focused, so they become well acquainted with the marketplace dynamics, knowing the key suppliers, buyers, and sellers, as well as the current and emerging competitors. They develop a strong industry network, which makes them efficient and effective in solving problems and creating new products and services. And over time, their experiential knowledge allows them to develop a sixth sense for their industry. When facing challenging problems, they draw from their own past experiences, interpreting results and applying pattern recognition to determine how best to proceed, based on their intuitive knowledge of what previously has worked—and what hasn't.

When I was a young marketing manager working for Pizza Hut Canada, I remember watching our division president, Gill Butler, ask probing questions, in our exact areas of business vulnerability, to our Canadian management team when we presented our annual operating plan to him and his staff. I turned to his CFO, Steve, and whispered, "It's like he's equipped with a homing device that zeros in on the soft areas in our plan!" Steve smiled and said, "That's his experience speaking. He's seen so much in this industry that he knows where to probe."

When Kellogg MBA students seek my counsel on career matters, I stress the importance of being very deliberate and choosing an industry with attractive characteristics. I advise them to use
two criteria in making a decision: seek to enter industries that are
expanding and have macro growth factors providing a nice tail
wind in their favor, and, second, pick industries that are undergoing technological disruption.

When an industry is expanding, it's a lot easier to get ahead
because there are more opportunities for career advancement.
Macrofactors driving future growth can come from a variety of
trends. There are consumer behavioral trends as seen, for example, in increased natural food consumption, which are helping
upstart food companies like WhiteWave's Silk soy and almond
beverages or Horizon organic milk compete against established
consumer food and beverage behemoths. Demographic trends
are another factor to examine. For example, the aging population
is fueling the launch of lower-cost and more flexible patient care
service businesses to improve patient health care. Another trend to
examine closely is consumer technological shifts, such as Internet
mobility fueling the growth of highly targeted and personalized
product and marketing services firms or e-commerce retailers like
Alibaba.com that are disrupting traditional brick-and-mortar retail
businesses.

A few months ago, a Kellogg student, Carl, asked me whether
he should take a job in the restaurant business as a finance manager for a leading pizza chain or as a strategic planner, working
for a health care provider. "Which industry interests you more?"
I asked. Carl said, "Probably health care, because it's undergoing
so much change." Then I asked him which job provided the most
potential to learn and develop his financial management skills.
"Well, each one should help me get better at a different part of
finance. The restaurant position will allow me to understand

financial operations while the health care job will allow me to understand areas like financial planning and capital asset allocation." Then I asked Carl which opportunity provided more career flexibility—which one offered him greater degrees of freedom in terms of his next move to aid his career advancement. "Well, given that the pizza business is in a slow decline due to changing eating patterns in the United States, I'd say the health care job offers me more possibilities going forward." I smiled and said, "OK, so what do you think?" He said, "I think I just answered it."

A primary reason I left Frito-Lay at the beginning of 1998 and went to Electronic Arts was because, at that time, the video game industry was poised for aggressive growth. Consumers were playing more games because of a nice combination of factors. Increased household broadband adoption was resulting in faster Internet connections, which improved game play. And hardware devices like Microsoft's Xbox and Sony's PlayStation were entering more homes, driving up demand for software games to play on the devices. Electronic Arts was feeding software games like *Madden Football* and *FIFA Soccer* into a quickly growing hardware device installation base. And the company did grow—during the ten-year period of 1997 to 2007, EA's market capitalization went from $500 million to $18 billion. (As of this writing, it is $30 billion.) Due to EA's growth, once I was inside the company, I had several opportunities for advancement—managers with sound operating skills were needed in multiple places. That said, although it made sense for me to move from the salty snack business to the video game industry, given the tailwinds EA was beginning to experience, I actually made a mistake in accepting the job. Once I was in my marketing position at EA, I realized that the people who got ahead—those rising into the most senior-level positions at EA—were avid gamers who had a deep knowledge of game play and user experience. Two of my talented marketing peers, Frank Gibeau and Chip Lange, talked rings around me when we discussed which games to bet on with marketing support and why. By having a strong working knowledge of gaming, they were more credible with the software game developers and also had a better nose for which games would be hits and which wouldn't. In one of my early performance reviews, I was told by my boss that to be picked for some of the big jobs in the company, I would need to rectify my lack of product knowledge by playing games at night and over the weekend. So I did this for about six months, muttering to myself every evening as I booted up games on my computer or put a game disc into my new PlayStation console. I'd stop and stare longingly at Richard Russo's new novel or an unopened DVD movie. It became clear that my interests did not include video game playing and I left the company a year later. Oops.

Closely tied to the importance of choosing industries experiencing growth is identifying industries that are experiencing disruption because career opportunities often arise from the changing balance of power as companies adjust and adapt to deal with disruptions. A new technology can shake the foundation of a company and send the old guard reeling—and looking for answers. "Does anybody here understand how artificial intelligence and machine learning is going to affect our durable goods industry?" Or "Should we be moving to a cloud-based SaaS (software as a service) model, too? It seems cheaper and faster and we're getting our clock cleaned by Salesforce.com!" Or "What's our answer to Amazon.com?! Now they're starting two-hour delivery on consumable goods and they're taking share from our retail stores." Whether you stake a claim in digital health care, education reform, omni-channel retailing, cloud-based web-scale IT, artificial intelligence, smart machines and Internet of Things, SoLoMo (social, local, mobile) digital marketing, or Internet security, it pays to work for firms in industries that are doing the disrupting, like Hulu,

Netflix, and Amazon in digital media programming, and not one being disrupted, like the traditional television and movie studios.

Gary Briggs, Facebook's chief marketing officer, emphasizes three factors when advising people just entering the workforce. "First, avoid too much job-hopping. Throughout your career, you'll need both mentorship and followership and you can't get either of them if you're only at a company for a few years. Second, you have to pick the right industry to be in. Trying to build a great career in a crappy industry—one where there are constant cuts and cost rationalization—won't allow you to grow personally and will hurt your career. Growth solves most problems. So take the time to pick the right business to be in. Third—and this is really hard—try not to worry excessively. You'll lose your energy and focus. If I'm nervous and worried about keeping my job or worried about making the wrong decision, I'll tie up. I will burn energy and will be less effective. So try to realize when you're in a state of fear and work your way out of it—talk yourself out of it. You can't let your fear control you."

Operational Ability—Knowing How to Do It

People with the right stuff are able to identify and focus on the high-leverage activities that will propel their business forward. They understand their company's operational value chain (the key business activities that drive customer value), where their projects fit within it, and the groups with whom they are dependent and need to align in order to succeed. They don't try to get everything done—they get the right things done and have the planning and organizational skills that the Whirling Dervish lacks. And importantly, they proactively establish a high-speed network of knowledge experts who help provide advice and support in order to complete critical tasks. There is a knowledge deficit inherent in every job and high performers are able to answer the question "What is the fastest route to getting the information I need to fill my knowledge gap?"

Over time, as a brand marketing manager at Frito-Lay, I carefully vetted and developed a very qualified cross functional network of experts to help me get things done. When I needed to understand if a retailer would accept the pricing on a new product my team developed, I'd call Kevin Vivian or Karen Sheinberg, two sales leaders, and they'd test the waters for me with Publix and Kroger. If I had a product supply issue, I ran up to the purchasing department and talked to Fred Merrill or Chris Braun. These folks came from all over the company—from manufacturing, product supply, field sales, trade marketing, customer service, research and development, and new product development—and were at various levels in the organization, from individual contributor to vice president. I was judicious in using them because I didn't want to wear out my welcome with people in my network. And I took every opportunity to thank them (often publicly) for their support and look for opportunities to help them with their own business projects.

In my early years at PepsiCo, when I was still in my twenties, I identified a group of rising stars who took the internal network concept one step further, quietly establishing a smaller alliance within their broader work network. There was a cohort of four senior-level sales and marketing managers at Frito-Lay who had all started at the company at about the same time. Over time they all moved into various field and headquarter positions, but they stuck together and looked out for each other. Amazingly, they all went on to become C-suite officers at various companies. I once had the opportunity, firsthand, to experience the power of their network. I was talking to one of them, John, thrilled that he was taking the time to chat with me (I was an associate marketing manager at the time and he was a sales vice president). I was in his line of sight as he walked by my work cube, so he said, "How's it going?" I said, "Pretty good, but I'm struggling with a sales problem." He said, "Anything I can help you with?" I said, "I am trying to find a sales territory willing to test a Fritos product line extension aimed at convenience stores. So far I don't have any takers." John said, "Hold on" and grabbed my landline phone and called a number. Three minutes later I had my test market. John winked at me and said, "A buddy of mine" and left my cube. I walked on air down to the lunchroom about fifteen minutes later. This made a strong impression on me so I mimicked it. Over time, I developed a tight alliance of work friends—one was in the finance department, another in sales, and two were in marketing—and we supported and looked out for each other. This network is alive and kicking to this day. For example, only a few months ago, one member of the alliance was struggling with a job move—should he stay at his big electronics company or take a flier on a very early-stage Internet of Things start-up? He tapped the network and we helped him evaluate the pros and cons of leaving. (He left.)

Functional job skills and operational ability are especially important early in our careers. As I've said, successful managers spend at least the first six to eight years of their careers developing their functional skills and gaining operational competency. Although these skills provide people with a path to senior management, they are "pay to play" skills and not the ones that, over time, differentiate the stars from the solid performers. The skills that do, the three distinctive strengths—taking the initiative, building positive relationships with others, and having a strong drive for results—were examined earlier.

The Five Derailers

The five derailers—interpersonal issues, difficulty building and leading teams, difficulty adapting to change, lacking a strategic orientation, and not delivering on promises—sit in the denominator of the right stuff formula and, if not addressed, act as a divisor that cuts away at a person's skills and competencies. They interfere with personal growth and detract from potential. Discussing potential derailers is a very important but uncomfortable topic, so it's often conveniently ignored by senior management and the sufferer is left to struggle until the problem reaches a boiling point.

It isn't always green grass and high tides for high performers. Having "the right stuff" doesn't mean these people won't flirt with or experience a derailment event; it doesn't mean that in every year they'll surpass their performance objectives. No—in the tides of business, people with the right stuff ride the inevitable ups and downs and experience good quarterly results and bad quarterly results, perform well some years and average in others. They receive negative feedback and are warned about underperforming. *But having the right stuff does mean that these performers have the ability to bounce back: to learn from their mistakes, make adjustments, take corrective actions, and get back on track.*

Looking back on my own thirty-year business career, I've received some tepid performance reviews, where my boss wasn't particularly excited by my contributions. I've also received a few sobering ones, where the message was "improve or else . . ." Over the years, one solution for me—a way I've tried to get back on track—was to look for the gold in the dark—to find something positive from the tough feedback, something I could work on that would allow me to focus my efforts and continue to improve, such as filling in a skill gap or sanding down a jagged point around my personal style. In a performance review in my early years at Frito-Lay, I was told I was "nonstrategic" and that if left unattended, it would impede my ability to reach a senior-level position. A day later, after licking my wounds from the feedback, I asked my boss who was viewed as being "strategic" at Frito-Lay and what they did that made them so. Although he gave me the names of two people, he didn't really satisfy me with his answer to the second part of my question. So I went directly to these people and asked if I could take each to lunch.

I asked Laura, a brand marketer, how she had gone about reinvigorating the Lays potato chip brand, reversing its low sales growth rate. She said,

> I always start a strategic project by taking my ideas out to the field to get feedback. I talk directly to the people calling on our retail accounts, the route sales people and account managers merchandising the grocery stores. They hear and see everything; they hear what's working and not working from our retailers and they see how shoppers are behaving inside the stores. Nine times out of ten, they can tell me if my ideas have any merit. So go out and ride on a route truck with our sales associates or get in a car with an account manager and call on retailers with him. You'll have plenty of time in between stops to ask questions. And you'll know if one of your ideas has promise if he lets you talk to some of his key accounts about it.

The second person I took to lunch, John, was in our new concept development group. He told me that he equated being "strategic" with a practice he simply referred to as "synthesis." Whenever he was given a challenging strategic project, he started with a discovery phase, which he initiated by writing down a statement of purpose (what he was trying to accomplish with the project) followed by several hypotheses statements, which were his educated guesses that attempted to explain the reason behind the current state of affairs. "For example," John said, "my statement of purpose might be: 'To reverse the flat sales trend on Sun Chips by year end.'

And one of my hypotheses might be that Sun Chips positioning has weakened with salty snack consumers—that with the increase in better-for-you snacking over the past few years, consumers are more tuned in to the ingredient panel and have a higher standard of what constitutes 'healthy snacking' and that's hurting Sun Chips' appeal." Then, to test his hypothesis, John said he pulled together a list of people to interview. "Just like a good consultant," he said, "I look to talk to a diverse set of people who have different views on the topic, from the end consumer to retail customers to external industry experts to people in our manufacturing plants to our R&D food scientists. I am very deliberate about the questions I ask. I draw up a list of provocative ones, and when I interview, I try to set aside my opinions and stay as open-minded as I can." John said he asked open-ended questions that couldn't be answered with a "yes" or "no" response and gave people a lot of encouragement so they would open up and talk. He asked people to tell him stories or give examples that made their points come to life. Then, from his interviews, John said he tried to make sense of what he heard by looking for patterns and then writing down observations that might inform his future strategic direction. "I try to answer a few fundamental questions. 'What is the end consumer trying to accomplish—what value are they seeking?' 'What's getting in their way?' 'How would they like things to be different?' If I can answer these questions in this discovery and synthesis process, I'm usually well on the way to being able to come up with solutions."

After talking with these two people, I started using their approaches in my job. I know their advice helped me, because in the following year's performance review, my rating for the competency "thinks strategically" was no longer "below target."

Another way I've gotten back on track after receiving tough feedback or encountering a career setback is by altering my fear-ridden mind-set by reframing the troubling situation in a more positive

light and then seeking out sources of inspiration to spark my enthusiasm and recommit to my work. To reduce my fear and reframe
the situation, I remind myself that negative events are usually the
best source of personal growth and if I'm committed to making a
change and recovering from a setback, I *will* be able to improve
and end up at a better place. I play old mental tapes that will give
me confidence. I remind myself that I was able to recover from
setbacks in the past, learn from them, and improve my capabilities.
I recall the time that I tore apart my left knee playing basketball in
a high school pickup game, had several reconstructive surgeries,
and was told by various physicians that, as a competitive swimmer,
I wouldn't be able to kick breaststroke ever again. I rehabilitated
my knee with tremendous diligence and ended up competing as
a scholarship athlete in college—specializing in the four-hundred
individual medley, a grueling race that required the ability to swim
one hundred yards of breaststroke. I also remind myself that I felt
completely overwhelmed by all the smart people at Stanford University, was nearly paralyzed in the classroom, which resulted in a
pretty average GPA during my first first year, but that I worked hard
to learn new study skills and recovered to post strong grades in my
final few years. And then I recall that, after I was nearly fired from
Frito-Lay in 1995, I learned to curb several glaring interpersonal
issues, such as working on my self-control with authority figures,
regrouped, and ended up getting promoted a few years later.

Then I try to seek out sources of inspiration to increase my motivation level and help me to recommit to my job. After the review
where I was deemed to be "nonstrategic," inspired by John, the fellow I spoke to in new concept development, I decided to become
more skilled at understanding how to create and field early-stage,
discovery-oriented market research—an important part of my
marketing job at the time, which was to increase Frito-Lay's salty
snack consumption with Hispanic people in Texas and California.

I read books to better understand field-based interviewing research methods. I shadowed ethnographic researchers from professional market research firms. I spent a meaningful amount of time interviewing consumers in interesting Hispanic communities in East Los Angeles, Harlingen, McAllen, and Laredo. I became very interested in Mexican culture and started reading more about the history of the country. As a result, as my learning curve steepened, I found myself coming into the office excited about the day ahead.

Mike Gamson, the senior vice president of global solutions at LinkedIn Corporation, said it well: "I've come to believe that inspiration is the biggest force multiplier that manifests performance. It's like a great relationship, where you ask, 'How do I keep love fresh?' People who perform well are constantly refreshing their careers by reinvesting in themselves. They're curious and are able to find new sources of inspiration. They seek out new challenges — new stimuli that steepen their learning curve that recharges them and gets them back in that discovery mind-set."

CHAPTER 7

UNDERSTANDING YOUR MOTIVES

A brilliant and rewarding career — one with the right stuff — has its foundation in understanding where your talents and vulnerabilities lie and what motivates you. Before you can lead a project, a team, let alone an organization, you must be able to lead yourself. This requires self-understanding, in particular the ability to dig deep and pinpoint the sources of motivation that inspire you to perform well.

Motives are the source of your energy. They fuel what you're drawn to, driving you forward and allowing you to perform well. Your personal needs are the foundation of motives. When your needs are met, you feel happy and energized; when they're not, over time you feel a deep-set cognitive dissonance and anxiety. You will then feel demotivated — detached and unengaged from your work. If, for example, you are like me and have an inherent need for autonomy and self-expression but are in a job that's rife with check-ins and a stringent hierarchy of approvals, you will wear down and eventually won't perform up to your potential. Or, if you enjoy working with others toward a shared goal but are an individual contributor who works in isolation, you'll have an affiliative need that's not being met and it will affect your outlook and eventually your performance.

A case in point is Margaret, a quick-witted, fast-moving, creative-minded thirtysomething marketing director who rose through the ranks in several early-stage business-to-consumer Internet companies. After the Internet market crash of 2001, with a sizable San Francisco mortgage looming over her head, Margaret decided it was prudent to seek employment at a large, stable company—one that lacked and needed her cutting-edge Internet marketing skills. She became a marketing director at a large consumer products company, overseeing their customer relationship management (CRM) function.

"I thought the move to a larger company made sense, not only because of the stability, but also because I went into an industry—apparel—for which I had a great deal of interest. But in short order, I was miserable," she said. "I love speed and variety—a good day has me working with many different groups across a host of urgent initiatives. I didn't have that in this company. I worked in one area—CRM—and while the scale of the job was big because we were a billion-dollar company, the scope of my role was narrow. And the pace of the company was excruciatingly slow. The culture was very affiliative and quite political, so to get anything done, I had to meet and get the buy-in from about ten different groups, many of whom had no direct role in my projects!" Margaret didn't realize the extent to which working in a dynamic environment, where progress could be seen on a daily basis, contributed to her job satisfaction. She had a personal need for autonomy and achievement—she was energized by being held accountable for solving a host of early-stage start-up problems, working without a lot of oversight, and she enjoyed working in an unstructured, fast-paced, chaotic environment where process and procedure was minimal. She was a self-proclaimed "stimuli junkie"—moving quickly from one problem to the next was intoxicating to her. When she left the start-up environment and moved to a large company, her career plateaued. "My motivation steadily dropped and I found that my can-do, enthusiastic nature—something that had served my career really well up until then—went into hiding. In my third year, I was told by my boss that I wasn't being considered for a vice president role because, while I was respected for my direct-to-consumer marketing knowledge, I wasn't viewed as someone who could 'manage large, complex cross functional initiatives.' I did a lot of soul-searching after that conversation, and I came to the conclusion that it wasn't that I *couldn't* manage large, complex cross functional initiatives, it's that I *didn't want to*—because with the word 'large' came a variety of other factors, such as 'slow' and 'politically charged,' which didn't appeal to my nature. The experience taught me that having passion for a category—in my case, apparel—didn't hold a candle to being in the right culture and making sure there was organizational fit. So I left the company one year later and went back into a start-up environment, where I work today, as a chief marketing officer for an e-commerce company that is growing rapidly."

Margaret had the right stuff—but she needed to better understand her motives so she could put herself in the right place to take advantage of her skills and talents. *By understanding your motives, you can make better career decisions, placing yourself in positions that appeal to your inherent needs and interests.*

Five Fundamentals

We're motivated when we work by the five fundamental factors of achievement, affiliation, power, autonomy, and purpose. Profiles vary significantly from person to person: while one might be highly motivated by affiliation and purpose and very little by power, another might be highly motivated by power and achievement and not as much by affiliation.

Achievement

Achievement is the need to constantly improve your performance and to accomplish challenging goals that are meaningful to you. If you're highly motivated by achievement, the chances are good that you prefer working in environments with clear performance indicators, where your progress is tangible and can be seen on an ongoing basis. You are likely a person who seeks feedback in order to improve and advance. You are probably a person who sets clear goals, organizes your work effort, and measures your progress.

Affiliation

Affiliation is the need for maintaining close, friendly relationships with people; the desire to belong to a group and to be liked, preferring collaboration over competition. If you're highly motivated by affiliation, you are probably a team player who is a good listener and sensitive to perspectives of others. You are likely skilled at building team spirit to accomplish goals. Your boss may see you as a good barometer for the cultural climate of the team or department and utilize your inclusive nature to further develop the team's esprit de corps.

Power

Power, the need for having an influence on others, can be expressed either *personally* or *institutionally*. People oriented toward personal power generally seek status and recognition and try to control others, while those with an institutional power drive try to organize the efforts of a team to further the company's goals. If you have a strong power motive, at your best you seek to empower others and work to accomplish group goals. You are effective at influencing others toward your end goal and are able to work through organizational hierarchies to figure out how to complete complex, cross functional initiatives. At your worst—if you're more driven by personal power—you seek work that has the primary purpose of further enhancing your position of power, thinking "What's in it for me?"

Autonomy

Autonomy is the desire to have control over your work and the ability to determine what direction to pursue. If you're highly motivated by autonomy, the chances are good that you prefer to have discretion over your task (you decide what needs to be done), your time (you determine how to spend it), your method (you figure out how to do it), and your team (you choose with whom to work). Having an orientation toward autonomy doesn't necessarily mean you'll do everything yourself—that you'll be a Solo Flier who is completely self-directed. It means you'll have a high degree of discretion over how you structure and complete your work: what you do and don't do; who to bring in, when, and why. As Seth Godin, author of *Tribes* and *Purple Cow*, said, "The art [of autonomy] is picking your limits. That's the autonomy I most cherish. The freedom to pick my boundaries."

Purpose

Purpose is the need to be part of something bigger than yourself. If you are highly motivated by purpose, you are likely drawn to organizations and assignments that have a guiding mission that connects your work to some social good that aligns with an important personal value. You are drawn to a place where the purpose is bigger than the product—a place that uses its resources and profits to offer assistance to those in need, a place that provides scarce resources to the underresourced. As Dan Pink, author of *Drive*, says, people who are purpose-driven seek companies "who use profits as the catalyst rather than the objective."

What about money? Why isn't it one of these five drivers behind our motives? Obviously, money is a motivator. If our pay doesn't allow us to take care of the essentials—like food, water, a roof over our head, access to health care and education—or if we feel our pay doesn't fairly represent the value we offer, then money is obviously a critical source of motivation. But if our compensation allows these essentials to be adequately addressed, then we become driven less by *extrinsic* motivators like money and more by *intrinsic* motivators like becoming increasingly skilled at something we enjoy doing—something we feel provides value to others and meaning to us. Money will still be a consideration, but it won't be the predominant reason we choose the work we do. It becomes one of several motivational factors and may evolve into being a gauge of our progress in an area, a means to an end, and not the end itself.

In a meta-analysis that synthesized the findings from ninety-two quantitative studies of over 115,000 workers, the results indicated that the association between salary and job satisfaction is very weak. The reported correlation indicates that there is less than 2 percent overlap between pay and job satisfaction levels. A cross-cultural comparison revealed that the relationship of pay between salary and job satisfaction is pretty much the same everywhere. The analysis showed no significant differences between the United States, India, Australia, Britain, and Taiwan. This is consistent with Gallup's research on engagement, which reports no significant difference in employee engagement by pay level. Gallup's findings are based on 1.4 million employees from 192 organizations across 49 industries and 34 nations. In a widely cited piece of research, Nobel laureate Daniel Kahneman and Angus Deaton reported that, in the United States, levels of emotional well-being increase with compensation levels up to a salary of $75,000—but that they plateau afterward. The takeaway: money does not buy worker engagement. The more we focus on our salaries, the less likely it is that we'll find work that appeals to our intrinsic motivators—satisfying our intellectual curiosity, learning new skills, working in an area that aligns well with our values—the very things that make us perform best.

When I asked executive coaches, human resource leaders, recruiters, and C-suite executives why talented people derail and why successful people succeed, the theme of motivation came up time and again. Executive recruiter Ted Martin said to me, "You must go with the job that is the right fit for your needs—even if it's not the fancy job. Otherwise you'll underperform and be tagged as the guy who gets coffee and donuts for everyone." Melanie, the general counsel at a midsized financial services firm in New York that specializes in investment management support for foundations, said, "My big mistake came from making the decision to go to a place that wasn't consistent with my values and needs. Earlier in my career, I worked at a huge, impersonal place that was a terrible fit for me, and I was in an industry—corporate and pension fund asset management—in which I had no real interest."

"When I coach people who are struggling," says executive coach Brooke Vuckovic, "I work with them to understand their 'drivers'—their values, motives, and needs. People who derail may have a mismatch between their job and their core skills, but more frequently they have a mismatch between their work and their drivers. That's the underlying problem. They're doing work they're skilled at but doesn't truly interest them or are in an environment that's not aligned with what they value." Brooke paused and then said, "The most important thing high performers do is figure out what matters most to them. Then they translate that into the work direction they want to take."

If gaining an accurate understanding of motives is a critical component to career satisfaction, what prevents people from pinpointing them and using that knowledge to make better career choices? The first reason is that motives are subconscious needs and harder to pinpoint than, say, our values. Values, the beliefs or ideals we hold as important, are easier to give voice to and make explicit. Ask someone what he values, and he will rattle off a few thoughts after a few seconds of reflection: "I value adventure and discovery—I love to travel and experience new things; and I really value education since it is so important to be well informed and understand what's going on in the world."

Motives are harder to explicitly express because they are latent psychological states, the underlying current of needs within us that cry out for actualization. So if you ask people what motivates them, the chances are good they won't have a well-articulated response. They might say something like, "Well, I guess I'm kind of motivated by money" but in many cases that's not a well-considered response. Money is usually a means to an end—a lubricant that fuels some other motive or need. Perhaps they're motivated by achievement and money is a scorecard that gauges progress.

The second reason why we have a hard time pinpointing our motives is that it's rare that anyone at our place of work will help us understand them. Has anyone holding a position of authority and influence at your firm *ever* tried to help you better understand your motives? Has your boss or HR manager ever said, "Hey, Karen, let's spend some time on your motives, so we can make sure you're in the right position—one that is aligned with your needs and is really fulfilling to you." Not a chance. In my thirty-year career, no one has ever—*not once*—brought this topic to my attention. I've taken the Myers-Briggs personality type indicator (a personality inventory designed to indicate preferences for how we perceive the world and make decisions) and the Gallup StrengthsFinder evaluation to help me understand my personality profile so I can work effectively with others, but no one has ever tried to help me better understand my drives, needs, and motives. Why would they? My organization doesn't want me to question what I'm doing (perhaps I'm in the wrong job or at the wrong company!); they want me to pump out work on the task at hand. Although that perspective may seem jaded, it's not my antiauthority, mischievous gene coming out to play—it's the organizational reality we all face. Although there must be companies out there committed to helping employees better understand their motives so they can assist them in finding the right job (even if it's in a different department, division, or even company), they are few and far between. If you happen to work for one, consider yourself lucky.

I spent many years in large, well-run corporations before I realized that I worked in environments that were poorly aligned with two fundamental needs of mine: autonomy and self-expression. Once, when I was around thirty-three or thirty-four years old and a director of brand marketing at Frito-Lay, I became faint and nearly blacked out when presenting to an audience. I had to excuse myself from the stage. Then it happened again at work a month later, when I was in a meeting. I felt my heart pounding erratically in my chest and I felt faint and had to lie down for a minute behind a conference room table. I went to a cardiologist who took me through a battery of tests and told me that he couldn't find anything wrong. I had a heart arrhythmia, but it was nothing to worry about. "I see this in guys your age, those in their midthirties," my cardiologist told me. "They're trying to do well at work. It usually involves stress. Is there a lot of stress in your job?" I responded that there was stress, of course, but "no more than normal." Not long after my visit to the doctor, I left PepsiCo for a smaller, more informal company (a fraction of the size of PepsiCo), and I never had a fainting spell again. I was holding on so tight at PepsiCo—self-monitoring my behavior, trying to fit in to the polished corporate culture, and acting "appropriately"—that it was taking a not-so-subtle toll on my health. This incident helped me to understand my motives and the gap between my personality and the culture of the company. It made a tremendous impression on me.

So how can you better understand your motives, so you work your way into the right job, in the right industry? Below are a series of statements to consider, which I developed based on the work of Hay Group and Harvard psychologist David McClelland, grouped around the five primary motives outlined earlier, to help you identify the needs that drive you. Examine each question and rate yourself on a one-to-five scale, with one being "not like me" and five being "very much like me." Then tally your score in each of the five motive areas and see where you rate the highest. This exercise may help you pinpoint your underlying needs and drives.

Achievement Orientation

- I work hard to improve my performance.
- At work, I prefer jobs that have specific, measurable goals.
- I accept responsibility easily.
- I get completely involved in the task at hand and don't stop until it's complete.
- I do my best in jobs that are very challenging.
- It's important for me to make unique accomplishments.
- I like reading self-help and instructional "how-to" books.
- In my free time, I prefer self-enhancement projects, like learning to code software or learning a new language.

Affiliation Orientation

- I go out of my way to make new friends at work.
- I prefer working on a team to working alone.
- I become interested in the lives of those with whom I work.
- I often help people and console them when they're down.
- It is important to me to be liked by other people.
- Many of the people I work with are also my friends.
- I like reading fiction, and prefer books with well-developed characters.
- In my free time, I attend parties and other social activities that involve family and friends.

Power Orientation

- It's important to me to get people to agree with my point of view.
- I enjoy running clubs and organizations.
- An objective of mine is to gain more control over the events around me.
- I am verbally fluent and persuasive.
- I enjoy offering advice to others.
- I like reading political and historical biographies.
- In my free time, I seek positions of leadership in the community.
- I attend prestigious events.

Autonomy Orientation

- It's important to me to determine my work priorities.
- I want to pick my team members versus having them assigned to me.

- I would rather take more time struggling through a problem myself than have someone tell me the answer.
- I am a self-starter with an entrepreneurial mind-set.
- I believe that it's my boss's job to clarify the direction, but it's my job to determine how the work gets done.
- I do my best work when I have ample freedom to run with ideas and projects.
- I like reading inspirational books with strong, well-developed characters.
- In my free time, I pursue self-directed activities such as writing, reading, painting, home improvement, hiking, and working out.

Purpose Orientation

- I can articulate my values and have chosen work that fits with them.
- For me to get excited about a company, they must embrace a cause that's greater than merely making money.
- If a company's culture isn't well aligned with my values, I won't work there, even if the incentive structure is outstanding.
- Business can be a tremendous force of positive change in the world.
- I like reading books that highlight the social impact that companies can make on society.
- I have read books and/or conducted exercises to help me better understand my own purpose and mission.
- In my free time, I volunteer and lead causes and events that are important to me.
- I like to discuss my values and purpose with others and learn about theirs.

Motives and Job Choices

Although we are often motivated by several factors, usually one or two are dominant. It requires self-examination and inquiry to match our dominant motivator(s) with a job position that emphasizes that drive. I am personally highly motivated by achievement and autonomy, and I am affiliative but fairly indifferent to the power motive, particularly as it relates to personal power. It's just never been important to me. So I enjoy and thrive in the position I currently have, where I split my time between teaching my own business school classes (where I am measured on my performance on an ongoing basis by the students taking my class) and working as a venture capitalist (where I set my own schedule, evaluating investment opportunities and meeting with entrepreneurs).

Several years ago, I met with a career counselor, because, having been promoted to the CEO position at Walmart.com, I was surprised to find that much of the work didn't appeal to me. I had really enjoyed my previous job, where I was responsible for managing the marketing and merchandising functions. It required a balance of analytical and creative thinking and enabled me to work directly on the product itself (not only the merchandise we bought and sold but also the "product" in the form of the Walmart. com website), and it also offered me the opportunity to work with fun-loving, creative-minded and driven merchants and marketers. But my new job as CEO didn't feel right for me. I felt increasingly removed from the product; I spent much of my time either dealing with HR and legal issues or trying to influence constituents like Wall Street analysts, technology pundits, and the press. My career coach had me take several psychometric tests (designed to measure suitability for a role based on personality characteristics and aptitudes) and noted that I was fairly affiliative and had a very high need for autonomy and a very low power drive, which she defined as "the desire to influence others to your own end." She said, "CEOs are generally low on affiliation and very high on the power motive. Has it been challenging to run Walmart.com when you don't naturally have a high power drive? Doesn't your current position require it?" I thought back on my last year as CEO—how I had spent so much time trying to maneuver, cajole, and exert influence on my peers in Bentonville (particularly the chief financial officer and chief information officer) to invest more money and resources in our Internet infrastructure and capabilities—and I answered, "Yes, this position requires it, and it's been exhausting for me. I'm not having much fun at all. I don't look forward to going to work anymore."

Before I was CEO, when I had the number two job at Walmart.com—managing the functions related to driving revenue, managing a big group of people, and making sure the trains ran on time and our product/service offering improved—I really enjoyed myself. Then I was promoted to a position that was less about driving operating results and more about garnering resources by using influencing skills, and I didn't find it nearly as satisfying. My previous job, which required a high achievement motive to beat our operating plan and a strong affiliation motive to develop the talented members of the Walmart.com team, appealed to me much more than the CEO position, which required a strong power motive in order to influence a host of constituents to invest more resources in Walmart's Internet business. But, because I didn't have a good understanding of my own motives and didn't understand the requirements of the CEO position, I took a job that ultimately didn't appeal to me. It wasn't a good fit—and a few years later, I walked away from general management positions and became a teacher and venture capitalist. (And I'm enjoying myself tremendously.)

Different jobs appeal to the different motives of individuals. You'll be happier in your career if you can work your way into positions where the drivers of job performance match your own inherent motives. For example, according to research by Hay Group, successful management consultants are typically high in the achievement and power motives and lower in the affiliation motive. Consultants are under tight timelines to deliver insightful findings to clients (the achievement motive), and they must have the ability to influence their clients to understand and embrace their findings (the power motive). Entrepreneurial founders usually have a very high achievement motive, too (they need to create and launch something out of thin air) but are also highly motivated by a sense of purpose (they're on a mission to create something that the world *must have*) and are much lower than consultants in the power motive.

By better understanding your drives and motives, you can work your way into positions that match your inherent needs. And when you find those positions, the chances are good that you'll perform well. If you want to delve deeper into motives than we have in this chapter, you might look into Hay Group's Picture Story Exercise and Personal Values Questionnaire, two tools that can help you pinpoint your motives and values and how they apply to your work.

Determining Job Fit

Mark Blecher, the senior vice president of digital gaming and corporate development at Hasbro, had this to say about the role the organization plays in a person's derailment: "Derailment can be about a lack of ability, but more often it's about a person's place in an organization. Companies are better at identifying personnel problems once they've occurred than they are at assessing *why* the problem has occurred or how to prevent the problem from occurring—the latter is necessary to preclude derailment. Many times the problem is one of fit. You derail because you're in the wrong culture, or your company and your position in it has grown into something that you didn't originally sign up for."

When I counsel people about important considerations surrounding their career, I emphasize six topics when evaluating job fit: passion and interest for the work, skill set required, industry characteristics, the company's stage and its culture, the commitment level required, and one's own personal vulnerabilities.

Passion/Interest

Is the job (and company) well aligned with your interests? For example, as I found out, if a person is considering a position at a company like Electronic Arts, they'd better be interested in gaming, because that's what is discussed there (nonstop). If you're considering a job at Gap Inc., you better be a dedicated follower of fashion or you're going to feel out of place. At Amazon.com, you better be inherently interested in technology and the ever-evolving landscape of e-commerce and retail. If you want to work at Nike, you better know who is ahead in the NFL East Division and who won the FedEx Cup in golf.

When it comes to the level of their interest in an industry, I ask job seekers whether they read position papers, blogs, articles, and opinion pieces on the industry and company they're considering. If the answer is "no," I would caution them about working for that company or in that industry because the people who get ahead in that business are doing that reading—and enjoying it.

Skill Set

Does the position align well to your existing skill set? By taking the position, will you be able to further develop and expand your "toolkit"? We are, as I've said, mechanics hired to come in with our tools and fix things. Do you have the right tools for the position? When I left PepsiCo for Electronic Arts, I had the brand marketing skills required to do the product marketing job at EA, but I lacked the gaming skills—I didn't have a good fundamental understanding of the user experience requirements inherent in good game play—which made me quite uncomfortable in my new position.

Industry Characteristics

Are you entering an industry that not only interests you but is growing and will continue to do so? It's a lot more fun, as noted earlier, working in an industry experiencing a nice growth tailwind than one with a headwind because there is more opportunity for advancement.

Company Stage and Culture

Is the company in a stage of its life that aligns well with your skills, your personality traits, and your motives? Early on, in the *start-up stage* of a company's existence, when there are a handful of people employed and the venture is just getting off the ground, it's essential that you are comfortable with ambiguity, as you'll likely need to shift your business strategies as your team searches for that elusive product/market fit (where your venture indeed has a viable product/service solution that serves a burning customer need). The chances are good you'll also wear a lot of hats, as you move from one burning priority to another. In this stage your company consumes most of your waking hours—it is a baby who needs constant care and attention. You sleep when it sleeps.

Or are you more comfortable a little later on, in the *early scale-up stage*, where the emphasis is on creating product/service demand by expanding marketing and selling efforts and building operational and organizational capabilities to enable the growth of the operation? In this stage your firm is like a teenager and you're creating the rulebook to guide its efforts.

You may prefer working for a company in the *growth phase*, where your organization is a strong, healthy twenty- or thirty-something and you're looking for ways to continue its growth and development—by offering new products and services and by entering new channels and markets. In this stage your company has become more professional and polished—you are executing against an annual operational plan and you have an HR department that oversees your professional development and reminds you of the rules in the employee handbook. Does this sound like the environment for you?

Or perhaps you'd prefer the *mature stage*, when the pace is less frenetic and you can focus your attention on a specific set of responsibilities on behalf of the company. In this stage, your company is a fifty- or sixty-year-old who is no longer suffering from an identity crisis (although it does happen when growth grinds to a halt—then it can be all-hands-on-deck while the company searches for a new identity). Your work–life balance is probably better than in an early-stage company, but you have to learn to be effective in navigating through the inevitable politics and bureaucracy of a larger organization. Is this for you?

Regarding *culture*, every company has its own unique personality. It was a huge adjustment for me to move from PepsiCo (polished and brash) to Electronic Arts (casual and game-obsessed). And I saw more than a few high-flying managers stumble when they joined Walmart and didn't understand and adapt to its unique culture of humility, especially the emphasis on the collective over the individual and the near obsession with the details of execution.

The best way I know to understand a company's culture is by speaking with as many of its managers and third-party suppliers/partners as you can before you sign on. Ask them questions like:

- What two or three things docs the company really emphasize?
- What are the unwritten rules of behavior at the company?
- Does it have a mission statement? How about a statement of values?
- What kind of person does well at the company?
- Who doesn't do well there and why?

When evaluating a company, people often focus on the tangible things like role, responsibilities, and salary, but they neglect to dig into the cultural norms of their prospective employer—at their own peril.

Commitment Level and Balance

What is the level of commitment required to perform well in the job? How much travel is expected? Ask people who work there—not your hiring managers but people who would be your peers. In some companies, a fifty-five-plus-hour workweek is the norm for managerial positions. At other firms, you could shoot a cannon through the place at 5:15 p.m. and no one would be the worse for it. How many hours are you willing to work? How important to you is your amount of discretionary time away from work, given the stage of life you're in?

Personal Vulnerabilities

How well does the opportunity line up with your inherent personality characteristics and with your strengths, weaknesses, and areas of vulnerability? If you're a reserved and introverted person, being a brand marketing manager at PepsiCo—when I was there in the 1990s—probably wouldn't have been a great fit for you. The position necessitated strong verbal communication skills—constantly pitching to senior brass, to retail trade accounts, and to people in other departments in order to solicit support and resources.

If you're meticulous and diligent and prefer working on one task at a time and have the tendency to become anxious or overwhelmed by ambiguous or fast-changing situations, you may want to think twice before joining an early-stage start-up, where you'd likely have to jump from task to task based on the issue(s) of the day.

The point is to take the time to understand your strengths and be courageous in acknowledging your vulnerabilities, so you can work your way into a job that matches well to your personal strengths and motives.

To discover what people do best, one leadership researcher from Stanford asked thousands of people about their "career best" experiences. He found that a person's "career best" has three common characteristics:

- The job/career experience taps into their true interests and passions;
- It utilizes their inherent talents and skills and avoids their areas of weakness; and
- In the job/career experience, they are able to add tangible value to the organization—they could see how their work was beneficial and tied to a positive end result.

When I look at my current position at the Kellogg School of Management (where I teach entrepreneurship to MBA and executive education students), I feel very fortunate that, unlike my previous CEO positions, I am fulfilling, or close to fulfilling, these "career best" characteristics. I have had a long-standing passion for teaching and counseling students and entrepreneurs; I am able to leverage my relevant background experiences and skills to advise them; I'm not doing work that emphasizes my areas of personal vulnerability; and I can see how my work helps students learn new management principles and obtain good jobs and helps entrepreneurs increase their start-up's performance.

This is the goal of understanding your motives — to put yourself in the position to do good work; work that utilizes your skills and interests and is inherently satisfying.

CHAPTER 8

YOU CAN'T COUNT ON "THE MAN"

The Cold, Hard Facts of Our DIY World

Stephen Covey got it right when he said, "Always treat your employees exactly as you want them to treat your best customers."

But there's a problem—companies often don't. They certainly are deficient in a very important area: ensuring that managers develop their team members. According to Michael Lombardo and Robert Eichinger of Lominger Limited Inc., a leadership development firm, "Of the 67 [job] competencies in our model, 'Developing Others' is 67th out of 67 in terms of managerial skills. No wonder the leadership shelves aren't stocked with a lot of skilled people. Many organizations haven't learned how to run the [managerial] development store yet."

This alarming finding comes from research on 360-degree feedback on more than six thousand people ranging from individual contributors to managers and senior-level managers in 140 coun-tries. Over forty-seven thousand bosses, peers, direct reports, and customers rated these workers on a variety of job-related skills and competencies. Not only was "developing others" rated *dead last* in terms of skills that managers have, but "motivating others" was rated fifty-ninth out of the sixty-seven competencies examined and "building effective teams" was rated fifty-seventh. You get the picture.

In my job as a professor at the Kellogg School of Management, I have the opportunity to visit with hundreds of bright young MBA students every year. Many schedule office hours with me to dis-cuss their career aspirations. A lot of conversations go something like this: "Someday I'd like to be an entrepreneur—either go to an early-stage growth company or start my own thing. But first, I'm going to work awhile at *x* [insert large Fortune 500 company or top consulting firm] to pay off my school debt and to get skilled. They'll train me in *y* [operations, marketing, etc.]." Then they ask, "How does that sound to you?" And I say, "Sounds good except for one thing: who is the *'they'* who will train you? The data shows that 'they' don't exist."

"*It has to be you*," I continue. "You have to have a 'do-it-yourself' attitude. There's one person out there who *really* wants to help you get ahead—there's one person who's truly interested in your suc-cess and well-being—you. You are the means and the end. You have to be the agent of your own change. No one else will play that role. Most managers and organizations handle management and leadership development very poorly. If, in your career, you have a boss who truly cares about your professional development, one who takes the time to work with you on creating and executing a tailored development plan, you are one lucky employee. Most bosses are too worried about their own hide to take the time to worry about yours."

McKinsey and Company conducted a study of seventy-seven large US companies, asking over six thousand corporate executives about their firm's talent development practices. Only 3 percent said their companies developed people effectively! Although 73 percent of companies viewed feedback and coaching as important to personnel development, only 30 percent rated their company as excellent or very good at providing it to their employees.

You cannot count on the man. The man will let you down.

One of the biggest impediments to employee talent development is not receiving clear and timely performance feedback. Delivering hard messages to subordinates, according to Lominger, is "number one in a survey of what managers hate to do, so employees do not get the feedback they need to correct performance problems." Receiving soft, indirect feedback that didn't register wasn't a problem in my sobering performance review at Frito-Lay in 1995. My boss, Mike, let me have it with both barrels. "You do not follow my direction. You are not engaged in my mission, which is the mission that matters. Not your mission—my mission. I don't want you on my team any longer. Given your behavior, the marketing leadership team does not consider you to be a high-potential manager anymore." Punch. Punch. Punch. And then the knock-out blow. Down goes Cast! Down goes Cast! I have Mike to thank—and I did at a later date—for having the courage to give me very direct feedback. His frank message was the catalyst for me to take action and address my poor self-awareness regarding how difficult I was for him to manage.

When I asked Greg Welch, a senior partner at Spencer Stuart, one of the premier executive search firms in the world, what impedes career progress, he said, "Right at the top of the list is not receiving timely and useful feedback. Employees simply do not get the feedback they need to develop their skills. Employees need frequent, timely, ongoing feedback and counsel. Even Rory

McIlroy, one of the most talented golfers in the world, has a coach who travels with him everywhere, providing him with feedback all the time." In fact, McIlroy hired a second coach—a putting coach—after missing the cut in two majors in 2016 and enduring one of his worst seasons with his putter, where he ranked 130th on tour in strokes gained in putting. He tapped coach Phil Kenyon to help fix what has historically been the weakest part of his game. "It just wasn't good," McIlroy said of his putting. "I feel like [Phil is] obviously the way to go for me . . . and hopefully I will start to see little improvements each and every week." The putting feedback must have been pretty decent, as McIlroy came back one month later and won the end-of-year PGA Tour Championship tournament and with it, the prestigious FedEx Cup, which determines the season-long champion on the PGA tour.

An entrepreneurial colleague, Craig Wortmann, shared with me what he calls "the world's most simple feedback framework," which he uses as a managerial tool in his sales consulting firm, Sales Engine Inc. "When there's an opportunity to provide useful feedback to a team member or to a client," Craig said, "I go through four simple steps and I do it right after the event occurs, whether it's a presentation or an important meeting. First, I ask 'What is one thing you think you did well?' Then I shut up and listen. When they're done talking, I say, 'Here is one thing I think you did well.' These first two steps build their confidence. Then I ask them, 'What's one thing you would do differently?' Then I shut up and listen. When they're done talking, I say, 'Here's one thing I think you could have done differently.' These last two steps build their skills. Then I am DONE. I don't pile on, providing feedback in multiple areas. People can remember and act upon one thing. And by keeping the feedback process simple and brief, I use it frequently."

I have found from both my research and personal experience that the importance of having a do-it-yourself attitude is particularly true for women. To be sure, a complex constellation of factors is at work when we look at the paucity of women at the higher ranks of organizations—most of these are beyond the scope of this work but remain critical for responsible executives to understand, such as organizational and educational policies that work against women, and implicit and explicit gender bias. What is pertinent is that, although the primary reasons for career derailment are surprisingly consistent between men and women, research indicates that women's careers suffer more than men's because women often underestimate their own skills and capabilities and do not "ask for the sale" when it comes to advancement opportunities. Candice Frankovelgia, an experienced executive career coach at the Center for Creative Leadership, told me that "the biggest career challenge I see for women relates to their own perception—specifically a lack of confidence regarding their job skill level. Women frequently underpredict how their boss will rate them. They think their boss, whether male or female, thinks less of them than they actually do. I coach plenty of women around clarifying their perceptions of how others see them so they can heighten self-awareness, gain confidence, and become more assertive."

Betsy Holden, an executive at global consulting firm McKinsey & Company and former co-CEO of Kraft, echoes the refrain of many women who've documented their experiences in leadership and as executives: "Time and again, I've seen the discomfort women have in strongly advocating for themselves and it holds back their careers. It's something I've tried to chip away at for decades."

Holden identified four barriers for women in progressing in their careers:

- *Structural*—Women often lack access to the internal work network that men enjoy. Research by Boris Groysberg, a professor at the Harvard Business School, showed that women face less acceptance in male-dominated workplaces and receive less access to internal mentors. To compound the problem, he found that women avoid developing close relationships with men for fear of giving the appearance of impropriety. One strategy that star women use to counter these structural challenges that can impede their careers is to build and utilize a strong network of external constituents— with clients, suppliers, former coworkers, and so on—to help them succeed in their jobs and also provide them with career flexibility in terms of future job moves. Groysberg interviewed one female star performer who said, "For a woman in any business, it's easier to focus outward, where you can define and deliver the services required to succeed, than to navigate the internal affiliations and power structure within a male-dominated firm." Nevertheless, Groysberg emphasizes the importance of fighting through these structural barriers to develop strong internal relationships. The research showed that "if you don't have relationships, you have no trust, and you will soon not have a job. It is important that women parlay their success, built on external relationships, into strong internal relationships."

- *Lifestyle*—When choices have to be made about work–life balance the burden still overwhelmingly falls on the woman's shoulders, resulting in lack of career flexibility.

- *Institutional*—There is a perceptual bias about how women should behave. Research shows that women have a much narrower band of acceptable behavior than men. The McKinsey executive Betsy Holden said, "A man can bang his fist on a desk, raise his voice, and swear to stress a point and be perceived as 'forceful' but when a woman does it, it can be perceived as being 'inappropriate.'"

- *Individual mind-set*—Women often hold themselves back due to their own inaccurate self-perception regarding their capabilities, for example, by not standing up for themselves. Holden said, "In general, women are less assertive than men in asking for things—not in terms of going about their job tasks, where they are just as determined as men—but as it relates to their own careers. If there are ten qualities needed to secure a new assignment, a woman will wait until she has all ten to ask for the job. A man will go for the job after he has five. Women worry about perceptual issues—being thought of as pushy and too assertive. Men don't. Women think: 'If I'm good, people will notice.' They find tooting their own horn to be distasteful. I'm always saying to women, 'You are the CEO of your own life! You have to go after what you want. No one else will.'"

As a boss, I also routinely noticed the barriers that Betsy Holden articulated, particularly very talented, high-performing women advocating far less for themselves for advancement and salary increases than did their male peers. During my time as CEO of Walmart.com it was common, during annual performance reviews, for my male direct reports to try and negotiate for larger salary increases and higher performance bonuses. But these negotiations about money happened much less frequently with my direct reports who were women. Even the best performers would take a look at the final page on the performance review, which showed their new salary and bonus, nod, and usually say, "Thank you." Meanwhile, the men would say something like, "Carter, you're killing me! I worked my tail off this past year! I led my team to monster profits. You really need to bump me up another $15K. That's no skin off the back of our massive company." But it was rare for even the superstar women to make counterproposals. Why?

This process of sticking up for oneself and "asking for the sale" is frequently made more difficult for women than men because of their having to deal with subtle organizational biases. Persistent biases such as the "double bind" conundrum (where women are confronted with two irreconcilable demands: to fulfill the conventionally feminine expectation of being nice, caretaking, and unselfish while modeling the idealized leadership profile of being decisive, assertive, and independent) makes it difficult to do what's already difficult—to stand up for oneself on personal career matters and "ask for the sale." Numerous research studies have shown that women who excel in traditionally male domains are viewed as competent but less likable than their male counterparts. Behaviors that suggest self-confidence or assertiveness in men often are interpreted as arrogant or abrasive in women and are frowned upon rather than rewarded. Women are forced to expend a taxing amount of energy trying to walk the fine line of "competency-likability" and must remain on this proverbial balance beam while self-advocating during performance review time.

Although I feel ill-equipped to offer advice in this area, I know of many women who have found success by joining groups such as the Lean-In circles or professional and executive networks for women. Business schools and professional organizations are increasingly focusing time and attention to both educate women on dealing with these biases and create and support women-focused safe spaces within which they can "iteratively practice" the identity of a strong leader and work to better understand the unique challenges they may face. These are valuable resources of social support, especially for those who do not have active mentors and sponsors in their organization. These communities can help to create strategies to deal with these unfortunate organizational barriers.

Eight DIY Career Action Steps

Because you are the only one truly interested in your career and must assert yourself to actively manage and further it, here are eight do-it-yourself action steps.

Develop Goals and Performance Objectives

You can't get where you want to go if your destination is unclear. It's your job to plot your job goals and lay out your key success metrics. It's best if you do this with your manager, but if he or she doesn't see this as part of the job, write them up yourself and then seek managerial input. Remember to set SMART goals that are specific, measurable, achievable, relevant, and time-bound. For example, I would not say, "Launch a new Tostitos product line extension next year" but would instead say, "Launch a new Tostitos product line extension by the beginning of Q4, generating $30 million in incremental revenue."

Solve for Blind Spots

The need to solicit developmental and performance feedback, both formally and informally, is a topic I've covered quite a bit. The best performers are always trying to improve by learning and adjusting. Get into the habit of asking for feedback from your boss, your peers, and your subordinates immediately after you make a presentation or complete a project or activity. Ask, "How did it go? What could I have done better?" Initially, people may be hesitant to provide you with candid feedback but if you continue to seek it, they will realize that you're sincerely trying to improve and will usually accommodate you. For example, after I derailed at Frito-Lay in the mid-1990s, I told one coworker, an R&D scientist named Richard, "Hey if you ever see me getting a bit lippy with senior management, would you mind tapping me under the table? This was—how shall I say it—an *opportunity area* in my last review." Dick laughed and said, "You got it, Carter. Happy to poke you in the ribs if you're impolitic." Another thing you can do is ask to go through the 360-degree feedback process. Although it's no fun to read about your weaknesses, the 360-degree feedback loop will shine a light on your blind spots. I still remember one helpful comment from my 360-degree review during my time at Frito-Lay: "Carter: save 'funny' for before or after the meeting. When 'funny' is repeatedly inserted in the middle of the meeting, it can be distracting." (I think I was going through a George Carlin phase at the time.) If your company doesn't have a formal 360-degree feedback program, conduct your own informal 360-degree review, asking the people with whom you work what you do well, where you could improve, and what you could do better to support them.

Reduce Skill Gaps

Create your own personal report card of key skills required to do your job well. Assess your current competency level. Ask others where they think you're strong and where you need further skill development. Look for on-the-job developmental opportunities to become skilled in your gap areas. Track how you're doing. For example, if you are a sales manager for a company selling software to large enterprises, how can you turn your new account-selling skills from a "C" to a "B+" or an "A"? Perhaps you should ask around and find out who is considered the best at pitching new business and ask to shadow him on a few account calls. Maybe you should ask your boss or a coworker to role-play with you—she can play the prospective customer and after you're done pitching, she can offer a few tips on your selling approach. Or you might want to conduct a little research online or find and attend a seminar on the art of the pitch.

Seek Mentors

Establishing a mentor/mentee relationship can be tricky; it works best when it happens naturally versus when you formally ask someone to be your mentor. Find someone you admire who seems to share your values and has skills and experiences in an area important to your career. Ask her to grab lunch. If it goes well, she likely will say, "We should do this again sometime." Then follow up a few weeks later and begin to establish a rhythm. It's also a good idea to identify four or five wise people who care about you and can serve as an informal personal board of directors. These people can provide you with feedback in areas such as career management and work–life balance. A few years ago, when I was struggling to decide if I should write this book and didn't have an understanding of the true scope of the effort, I turned to Dan Pink, author of best sellers *Drive* and *A Whole New Mind*. I found a way to reach Dan through a fellow Northwestern University alumnus. Dan had encouraging things to say about my topic—"There are a ton of leadership books out about what people do right, but not many on what they do wrong"—then posed this question: "Do you like the topic enough to spend *at the very least*, three years on it—a year to conduct research on the topic, a year to write, and a year to promote the book?" When I answered in the affirmative, Dan said, "Then as a next step, I would write a comprehensive book proposal. Writing the book proposal will tell you if you have enough material for a book. Sometimes, when you write your proposal, outlining each chapter, etc., you realize you don't have enough content—you don't have a book on your hands, you have an article." Dan's counsel was very helpful on both counts: about the time requirement (it's taken four years) as well as the book proposal. (I wrote a fifty-plus-page proposal, and, after doing so, felt confident that I had the material for a book and not just an article.)

Create a Learning Circle

Set up monthly calls with industry peers to share ideas, perspectives, and lessons learned. I did this in 1999, in the formative years of the Internet, when I was part of the start-up team at Blue Nile Inc., a company that focuses on selling diamond engagement rings to men. At the time, e-commerce was still in its infancy, so I thought it would be a good idea to create a circle of peers (e-commerce marketing vice presidents in noncompetitive business categories) to share perspectives and discuss business issues. During monthly conference calls, we discussed topics such as what advertising, design, and web agencies we were using and how our marketing programs were performing. And perhaps most important, we laughed a lot and shared our job fears and anxieties with one another. That was priceless—not feeling alone amid the hurricane of fast-moving, venture capital–backed start-ups. Our peer circle finished each call with a little game called "What outrageous thing did your VC [venture capitalist] ask you to do this week?" It was comforting (and stress-reducing) to laugh as we shared similar requests from our respective VCs, such as "You say it takes six months to create and launch a new brand—I want to see it done in 30 days." Or "Maybe you guys should put cots next to your desks so you don't have to drive home late at night to sleep." Although we had very competent and helpful VCs at Blue Nile, I nonetheless found their involvement in the day-to-day management of our business to be distracting and yet another component to manage. I was quoted in a February 2000 *Wall Street Journal* article as saying, "I wasn't prepared for the extent of venture capitalist involvement. I sometimes feel like saying, 'Oh, will you let me do my job?'" There's my antiauthority derailment tendency coming out—as well as my need for autonomy!

Codify Your Learning

Keep a journal; when you learn something new, jot it down. This will help you synthesize and reinforce what you've learned.

Journaling has been so useful to me that, over the years, I have filled over twenty of them. The most important of these is one I titled "Notes to Myself"; it is a collection of life lessons that concern my direction and how I want to conduct myself along the way: my values and aspirations, specific career and life goals as well as how to deal with my personal weaknesses and frailties. It's filled with quotes and lessons from great thinkers and people I admire as well. In each journal's opening page I challenge myself with this question: "What would I do if I wasn't afraid?"

Increase Your C-Suite Visibility

We are all social animals, and leaders at the top of your organization are no different. They promote people with whom they are comfortable. So find opportunities—such as volunteering to lead special projects and signing up for task forces—that allow you to get to know the C-suite folks better. Not long after nearly getting fired, I volunteered to run MBA recruiting for the Frito-Lay marketing department. I had to provide weekly recruiting updates to a host

of marketing VPs and coordinate several fairly high-profile recruiting events, one of which was attended by our CEO and his senior staff. We ended up bringing in a strong group of MBA students and I am fairly certain that this extracurricular assignment helped to improve senior management's perception of me for the better.

Become an Expert

Choose an area of increasing importance to your company (and of interest to you) and go deep with it. Do this to become a person sought after for your specific knowledge of that subject. It might be in an area where a market disruption is occurring, such as the effects of SoMoLo (social/mobile/local) in retailing, or artificial intelligence, or digital interactive health care, or sustainable energy sources, or the smart machines and the Internet of Things. Conduct a literature review, do your own research, attend conferences, blog about it, or read—or write—a white paper about it. I did this in the mid-1990s, giving a research-based presentation on the increasing number of healthy snacking alternatives and consumers' steadily increasing consumption of "good food" and how Frito-Lay should consider participating in this trend. I presented my findings to several senior marketing executives in our company, and, although (at that time) it didn't lead us to reduce the salt or oil level in our products, it further raised the awareness level of this macrotrend and its future impact on our core business. It also demonstrated to senior management that I was engaged and looking out ahead on behalf of the company.

The Organizational Face of Derailment

I would take the cautious view that, in this day and age, you not only cannot rely on organizational support for your professional development, you also can't rely on your organization to reduce your chances of derailment. There is an "organizational face to derailment"—organizations unknowingly play a role in enabling people to get off the success track.

It's not uncommon that employees deemed "high potential" by their organizations are moved rapidly through a narrow path up the organizational ladder. The result can be their inability to adapt when new job skills are required, as well as not having the time needed to develop a network of key relationships to assist them as their jobs broaden and become more complex. In "The Young and the Clueless," a *Harvard Business Review* article about this very phenomenon, the authors caution that "putting these unseasoned managers into positions of authority too quickly robs them of the opportunity to develop the emotional competencies that come with time and experience—competencies like the ability to negotiate with peers, regulate their emotions in times of crisis, or win support for change."

Companies also focus employees on short-term objectives, which doesn't allow them to develop a longer-term strategic perspective on the business. And companies can be forgiving of poor behavior by their high-potential performers if results are produced, which doesn't force these employees to address critical personal weaknesses and develop important team management and leadership skills.

The danger of talented managers derailing can be mitigated by creating an environment conducive to professional learning and development in three fundamental areas.

First, improve the feedback that people receive so they can see why and where they need to change:

- Develop clear performance criteria for employees, with specific goals and objectives and key performance indicators.
- Provide employees with timely and ongoing feedback—whether the message is positive, negative, or developmental in nature.
- Deliver the message with compassion, clarity, and tact—avoid waffling or dancing around difficult feedback and be very specific, providing examples to help reinforce the message.

Second, create a development plan to help facilitate change:

- Provide both resources and incentives for change and involve the employee in setting developmental goals, covering areas that enhance skills, deepen and broaden industry knowledge, address personal vulnerabilities, and further personal development.
- Develop reward systems that reinforce developmental goals.

Third, support employees' change effort on an ongoing basis:

- Provide access to role models and coaches to aid in employee development.
- Carve out the time for training and development.
- Encourage new learning experiences (new tasks and projects, new assignments, attending conferences, shadowing functional or domain area experts, etc.).
- Create a cultural environment where employee development is emphasized and managers and leaders are rewarded for making employee development an important priority.

Final Thoughts

The topic of career derailment is important—over half of all managers and executives derail! And derailment carries a huge organizational cost. The direct and indirect price to companies of managers and executives who derail can be more than twenty times those employees' salaries. Management failure, regardless of level, can be so detrimental to the welfare of both the manager and the company that organizations and managers need to become aware of the characteristics of derailment on a level equal to their knowledge of the characteristics of success.

I believe that workers' rate of derailment will increase in the coming years, because the context within which managers and organizations must perform effectively is shifting dramatically. Factors such as the increased rate of technological change, the dynamics of globalization, and the lingering effects of the 2008 economic downturn have forced companies to become leaner and flatter. And the business environment in which they operate is faster-paced and more competitive. As a result of these dynamics, managers have taken on more responsibilities with fewer resources to assist them, and they have been rushed into new positions without the requisite training, increasing the likelihood of derailment.

Although receiving performance feedback is a key component of reducing the rate of employee derailment, feedback alone won't achieve the changes needed to prevent it from occurring. It's hard to change our long-standing behaviors, some of which may have been effective coping strategies until we take them too far. My mischievous tendency was an effective way to blow off steam when I was frustrated by a micromanaging boss or the bureaucratic red tape of a large company, until I took it too far and alienated my boss and other senior managers. Addressing our vulnerability areas requires us to examine a number of factors that work in concert with each other and to establish a plan of action.

Below are six steps to take, regardless of the particular derailer that might afflict you.

First, Determine What Success Looks Like

You've identified your derailment tendency. Now what is your desired state? What does the "after" picture look like? What are you aiming for? When will you know you've arrived? I knew I had my mischievous problem at Frito-Lay under control when I received a "four" in "executive maturity" in my performance review (one was very poor and five was exceptional. Over the course of the previous eight years, I had never received a higher rating than a three). I danced a little jig in my office when I finally nailed that four, unlike prior years when I would have danced in the main hallway. I felt like a dark cloud had passed by and shortly thereafter was promoted from manager to director.

Second, Understand Where You Stand Right Now

What does the present state look like? Where do you stand now in relation to your targeted state? How far is the gap? You'll need to seek feedback from people in various departments. They have different work agendas and encounter you in different situational contexts than people within your own group. Your goal is to try to have as specific an understanding as possible of how you're currently perceived, so you know what you need to address and the size of the "from this to that" gap. If people are reluctant to offer feedback, you can nudge them by making a self-appraisal statement or two. For example, you might say, "Ben, I may have a tendency to be disruptive in process-oriented meetings. Have you ever seen me do that or is there anything else I can work on to improve?" By being self-critical, you've just given Ben the license to offer his opinion.

Third, Take Responsibility for the Behavior You Need to Develop and Understand the Consequences of NOT Addressing It

You have to acknowledge and own the derailment tendency. As the saying goes, "What you don't own owns you." Once the problem is understood you have to be motivated to make a change, and, unfortunately, a good motivator is often good old *fear*— fear of not getting the promotion you feel you deserve or fear of getting demoted or even being fired. Sometimes we all have to be reminded that actions have consequences.

Later in my career, when I was an executive at Walmart.com, there was a really talented operator on our team who was leading a big, complicated initiative. He was the smartest guy in the room and thought two steps ahead of everyone else. I found him to be very talented but his peers didn't want to work with him. I learned that he directed them like a traffic cop during rush hour. He had tremendous vision; he knew exactly what he wanted to accomplish but saw his peers as his supporting cast. He even saw the chief marketing officer, a person senior in level to him, as his support staff. Eventually there was an insurrection. No one wanted to work with him. Nothing seemed to change his behavior, so his boss came to me and said, "You have a good relationship with James—can you please try to talk some sense into him? I'm at my wit's end." So I counseled him. It didn't work. A few weeks later I became more forceful, at which point James informed me that "the big dogs at corporate back in Bentonville love what I'm doing." "But your peers don't," I told him. "People are asking to be removed from your initiative." Then James told me that maybe we need new, more committed people. That was it; I'd had enough. I told him that in these types of situations, I had a three-strike rule: the first meeting was to bring up the issue and discuss remedies; the second meeting was to discuss progress or, in his case, the tremendous lack of progress around the issue; the third meeting was to either congratulate or fire the person. "Are you clear on what I'm saying to you?" I asked. "We are at the end of meeting number two."

What happened next shocked me. James's edifice cracked and he teared up, saying he felt so much pressure to deliver on his big initiative and not let the entire one-million-person company down. After giving him some time to release the fear that had bottled up inside him, I told James he didn't have to go it alone, that we were all in this together and he needed to see his peers as his teammates. I told him that if the initiative failed but he went about it the right way, he wouldn't be letting anyone down and certainly wouldn't be punished. "We all signed up for this initiative—we're in this together," I said. If we got a base hit from it, fine. A homer—terrific. And if we struck out that was OK, too. We just needed to swing at good pitches—to have quality at-bats—and to play as a team. I think it was a pivotal conversation. The poor fellow felt the weight of this massive company on his shoulders and when he realized it wasn't his burden to bear alone, he immediately stopped acting like a lone ranger and pressing others so hard. His performance improved immediately. Tying a bow on this story: James is now a senior vice president at a Fortune 500 technology company. He called me last year—over a decade after our watershed conversation—and told me that our conversation was a turning point in his career. I received more satisfaction out of that phone call than I did with hitting any annual profit plan.

Fourth, Create Experiences That Test You in the Developmental Area

It's not enough to understand your developmental area—you must determine what success looks like and put together a clear and measurable game plan. You must then find ways to place yourself in on-the-job experiences that will allow you to develop new skills in areas that are underdeveloped or weaknesses. Think of it as developing new muscles and muscle memory that you can fall back on, instead of falling back on old negative behavior. For example, early in my career, when I was an assistant marketing manager in the Canadian division of Pizza Hut, I had a poor working knowledge of our restaurant operations and how our marketing programs affected them, so I spent time as a waiter and a cook in several Pizza Huts in order to better understand how our store operations worked and the challenges our restaurant personnel faced. That experience helped me tremendously. Later, when I was responsible for creating new marketing programs to increase store sales, I often drew from my time in Pizza Hut restaurants to ensure our advertising promotions were designed with an understanding of store operations. For example, when one of my coworkers proposed that we develop a lunch promotion that included a discount offer on two different product lines—our single-serve personal pan pizzas as well as our calzones (which we named "Calizza"), I advised him to promote just one product line, our popular personal pan pizzas, during the lunch rush, because they were much easier to make than Calizzas.

Fifth, Find People to Support You in Your Efforts

Changing grooved behavior is hard; you will need to find people to support you along the way. First and foremost, you want your boss as one of them. That said, you also need to enlist friends, peers, and perhaps a mentor to hold a mirror up to your face when necessary and to prod and encourage you to work on changing old behaviors and developing new skills. About nine months after coming close to getting fired at Frito-Lay, I came out of a meeting where I'd presented our new Hispanic marketing initiative to a group of sales and marketing executives. My boss, Stephen Quinn, pulled me aside immediately and didn't even bother with the "How do you think that went?" opening. Instead he launched right into it: "You were defensive when Compton [the head of sales] asked why the program wasn't already in a test market. You got lippy. Hello! The fact that he wanted it in-market meant that he liked the program!" Stephen then asked, "What should you have said? I want to hear it." I responded, "I should have collected myself first and told him I'll go back and scrub the plan and see how we can get it into a pilot market faster." Stephen said, "That's right! You just took a little step back in your progress." Then he turned and walked off. I knew my new boss had my best interests in mind and I felt worse about letting him down than I did with the way I represented myself in the big meeting.

Sixth, Create Methods and Reminders to Keep You on Track

Develop methods, guidelines, even devices, that will reinforce the new behavior you're working to develop. In my case, I used all of the following at one time or another:

- A rubber band on my wrist. (Mine, as noted earlier, said "Breathe" to remind me to pause before speaking during charged encounters.)
- A reminder message on the wall above my computer in my office. (For example, a piece of paper reminds me, when teaching, to "use fewer slides and provide examples!")
- An acronym that I've committed to memory. (Mine is "HILLS": **H**umility [watch for ego creeping in unnecessarily]; **I**mpulse control [pause, then speak]; **L**istening [seek to understand before being understood]; **L**etting go [learn from the mistake, then let it go]; **S**ervice [be others-oriented]).
- A few mantras that I say to myself. (One I recite, to avoid "peacocking," is "I go quietly through the day; I go quietly through the day.")

In the final analysis, the best way to avoid career derailment is to take steps to increase your level of self-awareness. What are your assets? What are your liabilities? Where might you be unaware and vulnerable to derailment? A lack of self-awareness is the single best indicator of a manager or executive's impending derailment. As I said at the beginning of this book, research has shown that people who have an inflated sense of their skill level and who understate their interpersonal issues are more than six times likelier to derail than those with a clearer idea of their challenges as well as their strengths.

All too often companies ignore the topic of derailment until it's too late, but their employees cannot afford to do so. Of course it's important to focus on developing your strengths, but towering strengths cannot overcome debilitating weaknesses. We all need to understand and mitigate our career-limiting vulnerabilities.

I hope, in writing this book, I've helped you identify and examine your own potential derailment area(s) so you won't be blindsided by them. I trust that some of the remedies I've offered will help you address them. Then you can continue to ascend and unleash your "right stuff"—by being a persistent learner who listens carefully and knows how to enlist the support of others, a person who adopts a mind-set of being "in a persistent state of beta," observant and questioning, trying new things and testing new approaches, knowing you can always improve, that you are an ever-developing work in progress.

"THE WRONG STUFF" DERAILMENT ASSESSMENT[1]

Following are five sets of questions. Each set addresses a different reason for career derailment, from having interpersonal behavior issues (i.e., Captain Fantastic) to not delivering on promises (i.e., The Whirling Dervish). For each question, circle the number that most accurately describes you and your current situation with respect to your career.

When answering these questions, consider that you're talking to a trusted friend. In other words, **try to be as honest and sincere as possible** so this assessment will be helpful to you in advancing your career.

---

[1] © Carter Cast, 2017. This assessment was developed by Carter Cast with the help of Sylvester Taylor and Dawn Barts of the Center for Creative Leadership (CCL), and is derived from Cast's and CCL's research. Please do not repurpose without Cast's expressed approval.

Interpersonal Behavior (Captain Fantastic)

1. When you think about performance reviews you've had or informal feedback you've received, how often has this feedback been focused on your need to improve your interpersonal skills (such as improving your listening skills or being less being defensive, aloof, or abrasive)?

Rarely/Never ⟵――――――――――――⟶ Very Often

| 1 | 2 | 3 | 4 | 5 |

2. Think about how you act when you work with others under stressful conditions. How often would you say you become visibly upset or volatile in these types of situation?

Rarely/Never ⟵――――――――――――⟶ Very Often

| 1 | 2 | 3 | 4 | 5 |

3. If you asked your peers what it's like to work with you, how do you think they would respond?

Very Easy to Work With ⟵――――――――――――⟶ Very Difficult to Work With

| 1 | 2 | 3 | 4 | 5 |

4. When working through business situations, especially those involving conflict, how easy or difficult is it for you to take into account your coworker's viewpoint?

Find It Easy to Look at Situation from Coworker's Viewpoint ⟵――――――――――――⟶ Find It Difficult to Look at Situation from Coworker's Viewpoint

| 1 | 2 | 3 | 4 | 5 |

5. To what extent are you reluctant to share decision-making authority with others?

Not at All Reluctant				Very Reluctant
1	2	3	4	5

Interpersonal Behavior: Add the total score from questions 1–5: _____

Managing and Leading Teams (The Solo Flier)

6. When your coworkers or people you manage get stuck or don't know how to approach a work problem, how often do you find yourself becoming visibly impatient with the situation?

Rarely/Never				Very Often
1	2	3	4	5

7. Thinking about the people you manage or others in your organization, how comfortable do you think they are in coming to you with a work problem?

Very Comfortable				Not at All Comfortable
1	2	3	4	5

8. Think about how you communicate your vision for the business with your team members and coworkers. How well do you think they understand your vision and what you see as important to accomplish in order to succeed?

Very Well				Not at All Well
1	2	3	4	5

9.   In general, when you are in a meeting, do you find that you mainly listen or that you mainly talk?

Mainly Listen   Mainly Talk

1   2   3   4   5

10. When faced with a situation where there is conflict among those with whom you work, how promptly do you help resolve the conflict?

Very   Very Slowly,
Promptly   If at All

1   2   3   4   5

Managing and Leading Teams: Add the total score from questions 6–10: _____

Adapting to Change (Version 1.0)

11. How resistant would you say you are when asked to change the way you do things at work?

Rarely   Very
Resistant   Resistant

1   2   3   4   5

12. Think about situations in your career when you've been assigned to a new boss. How easy or difficult have you found it getting used to his or her approach?

Very Easy   Very Difficult

1   2   3   4   5

13. How knowledgeable would you say you are on the latest technologies that are influencing your business/industry?

Very   Not at All
Knowledgeable   Knowledgeable

1   2   3   4   5

14. Outside of work, how frequently do you read about what's going on in your industry?

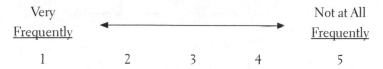

Very Frequently				Not at All Frequently
1	2	3	4	5

15. To what extent would your coworkers say that you're able to adapt to the personalities of different types of people with whom you work?

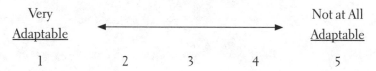

Very Adaptable				Not at All Adaptable
1	2	3	4	5

Adapting to Change: Add the total score from questions 11–15: ____

Strategic Orientation (The One-Trick Pony)

16. How would you describe yourself when it comes to how you use your skill set to address business issues?

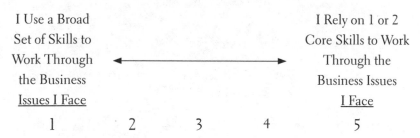

I Use a Broad Set of Skills to Work Through the Business Issues I Face				I Rely on 1 or 2 Core Skills to Work Through the Business Issues I Face
1	2	3	4	5

17. Have you focused on one type of work, holding similar positions throughout your career, or have you had a variety of work experiences, working on a diverse set of assignments?

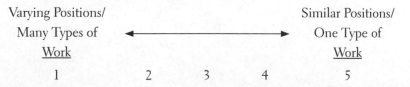

Varying Positions/ Many Types of Work				Similar Positions/ One Type of Work
1	2	3	4	5

18. How well would you say you understand the work and the priorities of other departments in your organization?

Very Well 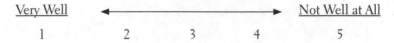 Not Well at All

1   2   3   4   5

19. How frequently do you receive feedback that you need to pull back and consider the big picture with regard to a business issue or situation?

Rarely/Never ←————————————→ Very Often

1   2   3   4   5

20. How do you think your coworkers would describe your level of knowledge about your firm's competitive strengths and weaknesses?

Very   Not at All
Knowledgeable  Knowledgeable

1   2   3   4   5

Strategic Orientation: Add the total score from
questions 16–20: _____

Delivering on Promises (The Whirling Dervish)

21. How often do you find yourself late on delivering against work deadlines?

Rarely/Never ←————————————→ Very Often

1   2   3   4   5

22. Given the ever-changing business environment that can sidetrack your daily calendar, how challenging do you find it to complete the priorities you set for yourself over the course of a given week?

Not   Very
Challenging ←————————————→ Challenging

1   2   3   4   5

23. How certain are you in your knowledge of what is most critical to accomplish to be successful in your job?

<u>Very Certain</u> 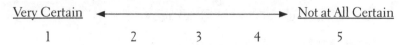 <u>Not at All Certain</u>

   1   2   3   4   5

24. How easy or difficult is it for you to say no to a work colleague regarding requests that are outside of your core responsibilities?

Very Easy   Very Difficult

to Say No   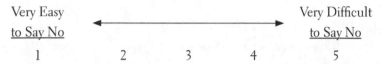   to Say No

   1   2   3   4   5

25. How often do you find that you commit yourself to a situation or course of action before giving it full and thoughtful consideration?

<u>Rarely/Never</u>   <u>Very Often</u>

   1   2   3   4   5

Delivering on Promises: Add the total score from questions 21–25: _____

Examining Your Results

When you are finished with the assessment, examine your scores for each of the five areas of potential career derailment. **The higher your score in a particular topic area (e.g., "interpersonal skills") or to a particular question, the greater the likelihood that this area may be impeding your career progress. Thus, it deserves your attention.**

Your score for each area:

Interpersonal Behavior (Captain Fantastic)

Add the total score from questions 1–5:   ____

Managing and Leading Teams (The Solo Flier)

Add the total score from questions 6–10:   ____

Adapting to Change (Version 1.0)

Add the total score from questions 11–15:   ____

Strategic Orientation (The One-Trick Pony)

Add the total score from questions 16–20:   ____

Delivering on Promises (The Whirling Dervish)

Add the total score from questions 21–25:   ____

Score 19–25: If you scored between 19 and 25 in any of the five derailment areas, you should **focus your attention** in that area to mitigate the risk of career derailment. You should actively work to develop a game plan.

Score 12–18: If you scored between 12 and 18 in any of the five derailment areas, you should **pay attention** to that area, particularly on questions where you answered with a "4" or a "5." These could be areas that could trip you up if not addressed.

Score 5–11: If you scored between 5 and 11 in any of the five derailment areas, this is an area of **little concern**. You appear to have this aspect of your career well under control.

Introduction

5 **managers and leaders will derail:** Joyce Hogan, Robert Hogan, and Robert Kaiser, "Management Derailment," in *American Psychological Association Handbook of Industrial and Organizational Psychology*, Vol. 3, ed. Sheldon Zedeck (Washington, DC: American Psychological Association, 2011), 555–575.

8 **flubbed a client presentation.":** Rachel Feintzeig, "Everything Is Awesome! Why You Can't Tell Employees They're Doing a Bad Job," *Wall Street Journal*, February 10, 2015, https://www.wsj.com/articles /everything-is-awesome-why-you-cant-tell-employees-theyre-doing-a -bad-job-1423613936.

8 **state of incarnation:** For more on this topic, I would recommend reading Robert Kaiser's *The Perils of Accentuating the Positive* (Oklahoma City: The Hogan Press, 2009), especially Chapter 2: "It Depends upon What You Mean by a Strength," by Robert Eichinger, Guangrong Dai, and KingYii Tang, and Chapter 3: "Managerial Strengths and Organizational Needs: A Crucial Leadership Gap," by Jean Brittain Leslie and Anand Chandrasekar.

9 **strong analytical skills):** Hogan, Hogan, and Kaiser, "Management Derailment," 555–575.

12 **doesn't do routines well:** Hogan Development Survey (HDS). "The Hogan Development Survey is a proven assessment tool that uses 11 personality scales to help leaders recognize shortcomings, maximize strengths, and build successful teams. The HDS measures a person's tendencies when under stress. It answers the question: What tendencies could derail this individual's career or performance?" For more

information on this assessment tool, see http://www.performance
programs.com/hogan-assessments/hogan-assessments-2/hogan-hds/.

13 **expected levels of performance:** Michael M. Lombardo and Cynthia
Denise McCauley, *The Dynamics of Management Derailment*, Technical Report, No. 34 (Greensboro, NC: Center for Creative Leadership,
1988), 2.

13 **and needs, on the other.":** Jean Brittain Leslie and Ellen Van Velsor,
A Look at Derailment Today: North America and Europe (Greensboro,
NC: Center for Creative Leadership, 1996), 34.

15 **career derailment event:** In our January 2016 survey of derailed managers, my team received survey responses from one hundred people
(forty-six men and fifty-four women) whose years of full-time work experience ranged from four years to thirty years, with a mean and median
of fourteen years. All had experienced some sort of derailment event,
resulting in being fired (47%), demoted (14%), or passed over for promotion (39%). Of the one hundred responses, ninety-three came from
individuals who are currently employed. Eighty-nine respondents disclosed their most recent individual annual salary, approximately 36 percent of whom had a salary of less than $75,000 and 64 percent of whom
made at least $75,000. Roughly 31 percent made more than $100,000.
We filtered for years of full-time work experience (at least four) and a
minimum/maximum age range of between twenty-seven and forty-five.

15 **they are usually wrong.":** Peter Ferdinand Drucker, *Managing Oneself*
(Boston: Harvard Business School Publishing Corporation, 2008).

15 **traced to relationship problems.":** Hogan, Hogan, and Kaiser, "Management Derailment," 2.

1. Captain Fantastic

21 **listen and learn.":** Marshall Goldsmith, executive coach, in an inter-
view with the author, October 2014. See also his book, *What Got You
Here Won't Get You There: How Successful People Become Even More
Successful* (New York: Hyperion, 2007).

21 **ethnicity or gender:** Examples abound. Here are just two: (1) "Leadership failure is a behavioral phenomenon," David L. Dotlich and Peter

C. Cairo write in their fine book *Why CEOs Fail* (San Francisco: Jossey-Bass, 2003), xi. (2) According to leadership researchers Jean Brittain Leslie and Ellen Van Velsor, who studied derailment extensively, "Derailment can almost always be traced back to relationship problems," in "Why Executives Derail: Perspectives across Time and Culture," *Academy of Management Review* 9, no. 4 (1995): 62–72.

22 **engendering trust.":** Stuart Kaplan, in an interview with the author, September 2014.

22 **along with them.":** Jana Rich, in an interview with the author, November 2015.

22 **and being passive:** These six behavioral traits were compiled from various research studies, the most influential of which came from research by the Center for Creative Leadership, Lominger Limited Inc., and from Robert and Joyce Hogan's Hogan Development Survey. www .hoganassessments.com.

24 **reached the NBA finals:** Mike DeCourcy, "Allen Iverson Regrets Being 'a Certified A—' to Larry Brown," *Sporting News*, April 4, 2016, http://www.sportingnews.com/nba/news/allen-iverson-hall-of-fame -induction-2016-larry-brown/4vgkkwbbbnre18xdk8umtx6tx.

25 **at the company.":** Raul Vazquez, in an interview with the author, November 2015.

26 **for the entire team.:** Brooke Vuckovic, in an interview with the author, November 2015.

28 **wasn't there before.:** Ted Martin, founder and managing partner of Martin Partners LLC, in an interview with the author, February 2016.

28 **and blind spots multiply:** Michael M. Lombardo and Robert W. Eichinger, *FYI, For Your Improvement: A Guide for Development and Coaching*, 5th ed. (Minneapolis, MN: Lominger Limited, 2009), 460.

28 **in the United States:** Cecilia Brooks is not her real name. I altered it at her request due to the sensitivity of the information she shared.

29 **that is still used today:** Three of Karen Horney's most influential books are *The Neurotic Personality of Our Time* (New York: W. W. Norton & Company, 1937), *New Ways in Psychoanalysis* (London: Routledge, 1939, reprinted 1999), and *Neurosis and Human Growth: The Struggle*

Toward Self-Realization (New York: W. W. Norton & Company, 1950, reprinted 1991).

29 **"moving toward people.":** Karen Horney, *The Collected Works of Karen Horney: Self Analysis. Neurosis and Human Growth*, Vol. 2 (New York: W. W. Norton & Company, 1950).

30 **interpersonal behavior problems:** See the Hogan Development Survey (HDS) for more information. HDS has eleven scales, or "dark side" personality dimensions, that measure how people behave when they are under stress. www.hoganassessments.com.

31 **to Horney's work below:** Joyce Hogan, Robert Hogan, and Robert Kaiser, "Management Derailment," in *American Psychological Association Handbook of Industrial and Organizational Psychology*, Vol. 3, ed. Sheldon Zedeck (Washington, DC: American Psychological Association, 2011), 555–575.

31 **have two or three:** David L. Dotlich and Peter C. Cairo, *Why CEOs Fail: The 11 Behaviors That Can Derail Your Climb to the Top—and How to Manage Them* (San Francisco: Jossey-Bass, 2003), xx–xix.

31 **own agenda over my boss's:** Hogan, Hogan, and Kaiser, "Management Derailment," 555–575.

32 **before acting upon them:** Daniel Goleman, "What Makes a Leader," in *Organizational Influence Processes*, ed. L. W. Porter, H. L. Angle, and R. W. Allen (New York: M. E. Sharpe, 2003), 229–241.

33 **very credible to me.:** Alex Moy, in an interview with the author, December 2015.

34 **react more productively.:** Laila Tarraf, in an interview with the author, October 2015.

34 **was wrong there too.":** Melanie is not her real name. I altered it and her firm's location, at her request, due to the sensitivity of the information she shared. The interview was conducted in November 2015.

35 **accurate self-awareness:** Guangrong Dai, Maynard Goff, Joy Hazucha, and James Lewis, "Detecting Derailers," Korn Ferry Institute, 2014, 3, http://www.hrpulse.co.za/downloads/Korn-Ferry-Institute-Detecting-derailers.pdf. Korn Ferry researchers analyzed nearly forty thousand 360-degree surveys and more than nine thousand self-assessments of leaders across the globe and compiled the results in December 2014.

35   **those of their raters:** Michael M. Lombardo and Robert W. Eichinger, *The Leadership Machine* (Minneapolis, MN: Lominger Limited, 2005), 58.

37   **give the Captain pause:** For a good overview of the 360-degree process, I'd recommend going to surveygizmo.com. Available at https://www .surveygizmo.com/survey-blog/guide-to-360-reviews-what-is-a-360-how -do-you-administer-360-feedback/.

38   **in their organizations!:** Peter Coy, "Ten Years from Now," *Bloomberg-Businessweek*, August (2007): 42, https://www.bloomberg.com/news /articles/2007-08-19/ten-years-from-now-and.

38   **with accurate self-awareness:** Dai et al., "Detecting Derailers," 3.

39   **Hogan Development Survey:** For more information on the Hogan Assessment System, I'd recommend going to this site: http://www .hoganassessments.com/.

39   **customer-friendly initiatives:** Morgan W. McCall, *High Flyers: Developing the Next Generation of Leaders* (Boston: Harvard Business Press, 1998), 35–37.

40   **strengths become weaknesses:** Daniel Ofman is a management coach and consultant and the founder of Core Quality consultancy. More information on him is available at http://www.toolshero.com /toolsheroes/daniel-ofman/.

41   **seeking in the conversation:** Michael M. Lombardo and Robert W. Eichinger, *The Career Architect Development Planner* (Minneapolis, MN: Lominger Limited, 2006), 22, 320–322.

43   **hurt them through overuse.":** Guangrong Dai, research scientist at Korn Ferry International, in an interview with the author, January 2015.

43   **new clients for his firm:** I have taken several liberties on this story, changing the subject's name and altering a few circumstances, in order to protect his anonymity.

2. The Solo Flier

54   **improve their performance:** I changed the subject's name to protect her anonymity. The interview was in December 2015.

55   **find the right balance.:** Ibid.

56 **and dampens innovation.":** Candice Frankovelgia, in an interview with the author, March 2015.

56 **to rely on others.":** Ruth Malloy, in an interview with the author, March 2015.

57 **senior manager's group.":** Eric Lauterbach, in an interview with the author, January 2015.

58 **allocating the workload:** Rajiv Chandran, Hortense de la Boutetiere, and Carolyn Dewar, "Ascending to the C-Suite," McKinsey & Company, April 2015, http://www.mckinsey.com/global-themes/leadership /ascending-to-the-c-suite.

59 **to dig her way out:** Jackie is not her real name. I altered it and several job attributes, at her request, due to the sensitivity of the information she shared.

60 **managing the individuals.":** Linda Annette Hill, *Becoming a Manager: How New Managers Master the Challenges of Leadership* (Boston: Harvard Business School Press, 2003), 284–285.

63 **how you made them feel:** Bob Kelly, *Worth Repeating: More Than 5,000 Classic and Contemporary Quotes* (Grand Rapids, MI: Kregel Academic, 2003).

63 **develop their skills:** Michael M. Lombardo and Robert W. Eichinger, *The Career Architect Development Planner* (Minneapolis, MN: Lominger Limited, 2006), 183.

65 **move toward confusion.":** Linda Annette Hill and Kent Lineback, *Being the Boss: The 3 Imperatives for Becoming a Great Leader* (Boston: Harvard Business School Press, 2011).

67 **the power of a positive no:** Kerry Patterson, *Crucial Conversations: Tools for Talking When Stakes Are High* (New York: McGraw-Hill Education, 2002); William Ury, *The Power of a Positive No: How to Say No and Still Get to Yes* (New York: Bantam, 2007).

68 **rules of the game.):** W. Chan Kim and Renée Mauborgne, "Fair Process: Managing in the Knowledge Economy," *Harvard Business Review* 81, no. 1 (2003): 127–136.

69 **about organizational matters:** Jean-Francois Manzoni and Jean-Louis Barsoux, "The Set-Up-to-Fail Syndrome," *Harvard Business Review* 76, no. 2 (1997): 101–113.

70   **for team members:** Brooke Vuckovic, in an interview with the author, September 2016.

70   **and useful framework:** Relly Nadler, "Are You Guilty of the Manager Misstep?" *Psychology Today*, May 25, 2016, https://www.psychologytoday.com/blog/leading-emotional-intelligence/201505/five-steps-improve-your-listening-and-empowerment.

72   **delegate and motivate.":** Stuart Kaplan, in an interview with the author, August 2014.

72   **and having autonomy:** Patricia A. Renwick and Edward E. Lawler, "What You Really Want from Your Job," *Psychology Today* 11, no. 12 (1978): 53.

72   **to do their best:** Daniel H. Pink, *Drive: The Surprising Truth about What Motivates Us* (New York: Penguin Group, 2011).

72   **and self-expression:** Frederick Herzberg, *One More Time: How Do You Motivate Employees* (Boston: Harvard Business Review, 1968).

73   **the right decisions:** Dick Costolo, in an interview with the author, May 2016.

75   **a shot of confidence:** Daniel Goleman, "Leadership That Gets Results," *Harvard Business Review* 78, no. 2 (2000): 4–17.

3. Version 1.0

83   **managers who derailed:** Ellen Van Velsor and Jean Brittain Leslie, "Why Executives Derail: Perspectives across Time and Cultures," *The Academy of Management Executive* 9, no. 4 (1995): 62–72.

83   **certainty to ambiguity.":** Kevin Murnane, in an interview with the author, April 2015.

83   **hiring filters for us.":** Tina James, in an interview with the author, April 2015.

85   **than situationally prudent.":** David L. Dotlich and Peter C. Cairo, *Why CEOs Fail: The 11 Behaviors That Can Derail Your Climb to the Top—and How to Manage Them* (San Francisco: Jossey-Bass, 2003), 43.

85   **boss entered the picture:** Adya is not her real name. I altered it at her request due to the sensitivity of the information she shared.

87   **and become vulnerable:** "Overdependence" is cited broadly in derail-
      ment research, including Lombardo and Eichinger, *FYI*, 5th ed.
      499–504; Cynthia McCauley and Michael Lombardo, *Benchmarks:
      An Instrument for Diagnosing Managerial Strengths and Weaknesses*
      (Greensboro, NC: Center for Creative Leadership, 1990); and Shel-
      don Zedeck, "Review of Benchmarks," in *The Twelfth Mental Measure-
      ments Yearbook*, ed. Jane Conoley, James Impara, and Linda Murphy
      (Lincoln, NE: Buros Institute of Mental Measurements, 1995).

89   **Andrew Wilson, who had just come in as CEO:** Ian Sherr, "Five Ways
      Electronic Arts Got Back in the Game," *CNET*, June 2, 2015, http:
      //www.cnet.com/news/five-ways-electronic-arts-got-back-into-the-game/.

90   **to an online content delivery service," Wilson said:** John Kehoe,
      "Electronic Arts Boss Andrew Wilson Is One of Australia's Top Global
      CEOs," *Financial Review*, January 9, 2016, http://www.afr.com
      /technology/electronic-arts-boss-andrew-wilson-is-one-of-australias-top
      -global-ceos-20160103-glym9s.

90   **we operate as a single organization.":** Andy Meek, "Electronic Arts' CEO
      on Transforming the 'Worst Company in the U.S.,'" *FastCompany*, Novem-
      ber 7, 2014, http://www.fastcompany.com/3038121/innovation-agents
      /electronic-arts-ceo-on-transforming-the-worst-company-in-the-us.

90   **as part of the strategic changes:** Chris Morris, "Electronic Arts Hit
      with More Layoffs," *CNBC*, April 25, 2013, http://www.cnbc.com
      /id/100675226.

91   **people who weren't thinking about players—a.k.a. EA's customers—
      first:** Adam Lashinsky, "How Electronic Arts Revived Itself," *Fortune*, July
      14, 2015, http://fortune.com/2015/07/14/electronics-arts-games-revival/.

91   **"I hope we never appear on that list again, I truly do.":** Chris Morran,
      "EA CEO: We Don't Want to Win Worst Company Award for 3rd Time,"
      Consumerist, September 5, 2014, https://consumerist.com/2014/09/05
      /ea-ceo-we-dont-want-to-win-worst-company-award-for-3rd-time/.

91   **As long as I draw breath, this will not happen again.'":** Ian Sherr,
      "How Electronic Arts Stopped Being the Worst Company in
      America," *CNET*, June 2, 2015, http://www.cnet.com/news/how
      -electronic-arts-stopped-being-the-worst-company-in-america/.

92   **learn so he could understand how to be effective in it:** Laura Flana-
      gan, in an interview with the author, August 2015.

93 **not allowing oneself to be deflected by the facts.":** Barbara Wertheim Tuchman, *The March of Folly: From Troy to Vietnam* (New York: Random House Incorporated, 1985).

93 **the solution to "wood-headedness.":** Michael M. Lombardo and Robert W. Eichinger, "High Potentials as High Learners," *Human Resource Management* 39, no. 4 (2000): 321–329.

93 **accommodate challenges to their knowledge base:** Robert Kaiser and S. Bartholomew Craig, *"How Is Executive Success Different?"* Paper presented at the Society for Industrial and Organizational Psychology's Fall Consortium, St. Louis, MO, October 28, 2005. See also Nicky Dries, Tim Vantilborgh, and Roland Pepermans, "High Potential Identification: Examining the Developmental Perspective," *Personnel Review* 41, no. 3 (2010).

93 **in more career promotions:** Kenneth P. De Meuse, "What's Smarter Than IQ?" *Korn/Ferry Institute Proof Point* (2011): 1–2.

93 **he or she received:** Cynthia D. McCauley, "Leader Training and Development," in *The Nature of Organizational Leadership: Understanding the Performance Imperatives Confronting Today's Leaders*, ed. Stephen J. Zaccaro and Richard J. Klimoski (San Francisco: Jossey-Bass, 2001), 347–383. Also see De Meuse, "What's Smarter Than IQ?" 1–2.

95 **you're going to find yourself in real trouble.":** Mike Gamson, in an interview with the author, January 2016.

98 **won't necessarily make you successful in the future.":** David L. Dotlich, James L. Noel, and Norman Walker, *Leadership Passages: The Personal and Professional Transitions That Make or Break a Leader* (San Francisco: Jossey-Bass, 2004).

98 **transitions that we go through when progressing in our careers:** Ram Charan, Stephen Drotter, and James Noel, *The Leadership Pipeline: How to Build the Leadership Powered Company*, 2nd. ed. (Hoboken, NJ: John Wiley and Sons, 2011), 15–31. In this book, Charan et al. identify six management/leadership transitions. I have simplified their work into four key transitions and added my own comments and examples to illustrate the principles in action. Also, in *Leadership Passages*, Dotlich, Noel, and Walker identified thirteen situations that involve transitional passages. They are: (1) joining a company; (2) moving into a leadership role; (3) accepting a stretch assignment; (4) assuming responsibility for

a business; (5) dealing with a significant failure; (6) coping with a bad boss and competitive peers; (7) losing your job or being passed over for a promotion; (8) being part of an acquisition or merger; (9) living in a different country or culture; (10) finding a meaningful balance between work and family; (11) letting go of ambition (to focus exclusively on what you do well); (12) facing personal upheaval; and (13) losing faith in the system (and overcoming disillusionment).

102 **I'm going to just shut up and listen to you.":** Marshall Goldsmith does a fine job of laying out this process in his best-selling book, *What Got You Here Won't Get You There: How Successful People Become Even More Successful* (New York: Hyperion, 2007).

4. The One-Trick Pony

112 **adjacent departments on which you have dependencies:** King Y. Tang and Guangrong Dai, *The Leadership Architect 2013 Global Norms. Report 2: Career Stallers and Stoppers Norms and Analysis* (Korn Ferry International, 2013), 3.

114 **lateral assignments that will broaden their perspective:** Signe Spencer and Chris Watkin, "Potential—For What?" Hay Group, 2006, 11.

114 **A single skill is never enough.":** Michael M. Lombardo and Robert W. Eichinger, *FYI, For Your Improvement: A Guide for Development and Coaching,* 5th ed. (Minneapolis, MN: Lominger Limited, 2009), 506.

114 **who thought beyond the specific projects under their jurisdiction:** Names were changed or withheld in this interview due to the sensitive nature of the discussion. The interview with the subject was in December 2015.

117 **delighted customers and a thriving business:** For more on value chain activities inside the firm, I would recommend Michael Porter's influential book *Competitive Advantage: Creating and Sustaining Superior Performance* (New York: FreePress, 1985).

120 **if they achieve short-term results:** Morgan W. McCall, *High Flyers: Developing the Next Generation of Leaders* (Boston: Harvard Business Press, 1998), 54–55.

120 **The guy was overly focused on getting to the next level:** Brock Leach, in an interview with the author, June 2016.

122 **working backwards as to how to get there:** Michael Luecht, chief executive officer of ML Realty Partners, in an interview with the author, December 2015.

123 **the company's critical work flow:** For more information on this process, I would recommend reading Porter's book *Competitive Advantage: Creating and Sustaining Superior Performance* (New York: FreePress, 1985), chapter 2 "The Value Chain and Competitive Advantage."

126 **the project was shuttered pretty quickly:** Names withheld in this interview due to the sensitive nature of the discussion. Interview was conducted in June 2016.

127 **"What skills do really well-rounded marketers have?":** Philip Kotler, *Marketing Management*, 11th ed. (Upper Saddle River, NJ: Prentice Hall, 2003).

130 **Books:** http://favobooks.com/.

132 **I get my hands on stuff and play.":** Dick Costolo, in an interview with the author, May 2016.

5. The Whirling Dervish

137 **you do what you say you're going to do.":** Jamie Dimon at the JPMorgan and Chase Founders Forum, May 27, 2015.

138 **though hers manifested differently than Bill's:** I have changed the name of the coach and subject I interviewed due to the sensitive nature of the discussion. The interview was conducted in January 2016.

140 **which leads them to make commitments they fail to keep.:** In *FYI, For Your Improvement: A Guide for Development and Coaching*, 5th ed. (Minneapolis, MN: Lominger Limited, 2009), 423, Michael Lombardo and Robert Eichinger list this propensity as a reason for derailment.

140 **they pick up a shovel and dig:** Mark Blecher, in an interview with the author, January 2016. I changed the subject's name to maintain his anonymity.

141 **prioritize, plan, and execute their work:** An example of a popular heuristic is the time management matrix that Stephen Covey popularized in *The Seven Habits of Highly Effective People* (New York: FreePress, 2004) and *First Things First*, with A. Roger Merrill and Rebecca R. Merrill (New York: Fireside, 1994).

142 **I doubt she'll be around much longer:** I changed the subject's name in this interview due to the sensitive nature of the discussion. The interview was conducted in November 2015.

146 **now I QA everything to death:** Interview with John (last name withheld due to the sensitive nature of the discussion) in February 2016.

149 **his follow-up book, *Making It All Work*:** David Allen, *Making It All Work: Winning at the Game of Work and the Business of Life* (New York: Penguin Books, 2008), and *Getting Things Done: The Art of Stress-Free Productivity* (New York: Penguin Books, 2002).

151 **Second, learn how to turn a request into a five-minute favor:** Adam Grant talks about this approach in his best-selling book, *Give and Take: Why Helping Others Drives Our Success* (New York: Penguin Books, 2013).

153 **In some cases, they made career changes:** This came from a January 2016 survey of one hundred derailed managers (forty-six men and fifty-four women) whose years of full-time work experience ranged from four years to thirty years, with a mean and median of fourteen years. All had experienced some sort of derailment event, resulting in being fired (47%), demoted (14%), or passed over for promotion (39%). Of the one hundred responses, ninety-three came from individuals that are currently employed. Eighty-nine respondents disclosed their most recent individual annual salary, approximately 36 percent of whom had a salary of less than $75,000, and 64 percent of whom made at least $75,000. Roughly 31 percent made more than $100,000. We filtered for years of full-time work experience (at least four) and minimum/maximum age range of between twenty-seven and forty-five.

153 **I learn about myself from the whole debacle.":** Ibid.

6. The Right Stuff

157 **raw intelligence:** John E. Hunter and Ronda F. Hunter, "Validity and Utility of Alternative Predictors of Job Performance," *Psychological Bulletin* 96, no. 1 (1984): 72. Also Frank L. Schmidt, "The Role of General Cognitive Ability and Job Performance: Why There Cannot Be a Debate," *Human Performance* 15, no. 1–2 (2002): 187–210.

160 **than I do in theirs:** Dan Marriott, in an interview with the author, August 2016.

161 **good hand in life:** Dan Marriott, in an interview with the author, August 2016.

161 **out by an organization:** Lyle M. Spencer and Signe M. Spencer, *Competence at Work: Models for Superior Performance* (Hoboken, NJ: Wiley, 1993).

162 **and management:** Robert B. Kaiser, ed., "It Depends upon What You Mean by a Strength," in *The Perils of Accentuating the Positive* (Tulsa, OK: Hogan Press, 2009), 15–16.

164 **outcomes of the group:** This is based on research from a variety of sources: from Robert Eichinger and Michael Lombardo, primarily "The 6Qs of Leadership—A Blueprint for Enduring Success at the Top" (Lominger Limited Inc., http://leadershipall.com/wp-content /uploads/2012/12/The-6Qs-Of-Leadership.pdf); from the Hay Group, particularly the research paper "Potential—for What?" (https://www .haygroup.com/downloads/pl/misc/potential_for_what_uk.pdf); from Robert E. Kelly's book *How to Be a Star Performer at Work: 9 Breakthrough Strategies You Need to Succeed* (New York: Three Rivers Press, 1999); and from John Zenger and Joe Folkman's research covered in their book *The Extraordinary Leader: Turning Good Managers into Great Leaders* (New York: McGraw-Hill, 2009).

165 **"having a growth mindset.":** Carol Dweck, *Mindset: The New Psychology of Success* (New York: Random House, 2006).

167 **"manages conflict effectively.":** Eichinger and Lombardo,"The 6Qs of Leadership," http://leadershipall.com/wp-content/uploads/2012/12 /The-6Qs-Of-Leadership.pdf.

167 **plan for them.:** Harry Kraemer, in an interview with the author, October 2015.

168 **persuasive with others:** Daniel Goleman in particular has done a great deal of research on this topic. For an overview, see his article, "Leadership That Gets Results," *Harvard Business Review*, March–April 2000, https://hbr.org/2000/03/leadership-that-gets-results.

168 **the conversation forward.":** Greg Welch, in an interview with the author, November 2015.

169 **point of view:** Brock Leach, in an interview with the author, November 2015.

169 **interpersonal skills.":** Laura Flanagan, in an interview with the author, August 2015.

170 **others' perspectives.":** Ruth Malloy, in an interview with the author, March 2015.

170 **"We did this ourselves.":** Lao Tsu, *Tao Te Ching,* https://www.amazon .com/Tao-Te-Ching-Text-Only/dp/0679724346.

171 **personal indictment:** Angela Lee Duckworth has done a great deal of research on this topic. She defines grit as "sticking with things over the very long term until you master them." She says, "The gritty individual approaches achievement as a marathon; his or her advantage is stamina." Her research found that grit may be *the* best predictor of a person's future success. Here she is in a 2013 TED talk: https://www.ted.com /talks/angela_lee_duckworth_the_key_to_success_grit?language=en. For more, see Angela L. Duckworth, Christopher Peterson, Michael D. Matthews, and Dennis R. Kelly, "Grit: Perseverance and Passion for Long-Term Goals," *Journal of Personality and Social Psychology* 92, no. 6 (2007): 1087.

172 **drive to succeed?":** Doug Kush, in an interview with the author, May 2015.

172 **having the right stuff:** This formula was inspired, in part, by work from the Hay Group (in "Potential—for What") as well as work by Michael Lombardo and Robert Eichinger in "The 6 Qs of Leadership," http: //leadershipall.com/wp-content/uploads/2012/12/The-6Qs-Of -Leadership.pdf, and "High Potentials as High Learners," *Human Resource Management* 39, no. 4 (2000): 321–329.

181 **fear control you.":** Gary Briggs, in an interview with the author, November 2014.

182 **knowledge gap?":** Robert E. Kelly talks about the importance of establishing this knowledge network in his excellent book *How to Be a Star Performer at Work: 9 Breakthrough Strategies You Need to Succeed* (New York: Three Rivers Press, 1999).

183 **out for each other:** On this topic of an alliance network, I highly recommend Adam Grant's fine book *Give and Take: A Revolutionary Approach to Success* (New York: Viking, 2013).

183 **the solid performers:** Eichinger and Lombardo, "The 6Qs of Leadership," http://leadershipall.com/wp-content/uploads/2012/12/The-6Qs -Of-Leadership.pdf.

188 **back in that discovery mind-set":** Mike Gamson, in an interview with the author, January 2016.

7. Understanding Your Motives

190 **Internet companies:** I have taken a few liberties in this interview, changing the subject's name and altering a few circumstances in order to protect her anonymity.

191 **autonomy, and purpose:** This is based on David McClelland's work at Harvard on need theory—see his book *The Achieving Society* (New York: D. Van Nostrand Company Inc., 1961) for more information— as well as Daniel Pink's book *Drive: The Surprising Truth about What Motivates Us* (New York: Riverhead Books, 2011).

193 **with whom to work):** Pink, *Drive*, 207.

193 **pick my boundaries.":** Ibid., 95. Seth Godin, *Tribes: We Need You to Lead Us* (New York: Penguin Books, 2008); and Seth Godin, *Purple Cow: Transform Your Business by Being Remarkable* (New York: Penguin Books, 2009).

194 **than the objective.":** Pink, *Drive*, 137.

195 **49 industries and 34 nations:** Tomas Chamorro-Premuzic, "Does Money Really Affect Motivation? A Review of the Research," *Harvard Business Review*, April 10, 2013.

195 **they plateau afterward:** http://www.pnas.org/content/107/38/16489 .abstract.

195 **donuts for everyone.":** Ted Martin, founder and managing partner of Martin Partners LLC, in an interview with the author, February 2016.

195 **had no real interest.":** I have changed the subject's name in order to protect her anonymity. The interview was conducted in November 2015.

196 **direction they want to take.":** Brooke Vuckovic, in an interview with the author, November 2015.

198 **needs that drive you:** Portions of this material came from the Hay Group in its work with David McClelland on motivations.

198 **underlying needs and drives:** Adapted from R. Steers and D. Braunstein, "A Behaviorally Based Measure of Manifest Needs in Work-Settings," *Journal of Vocational Behavior* (October 1976): 254. I also received excellent counsel from Hay Group consultant Smruti Rajagopalan on better understanding one's motives.

202 **to your own end.":** I took the Hogan Personality Inventory, the Hogan Development Survey, the Riso-Hudson Enneagram Type Indicator (RHETI), and the Hay Group Picture Story Exercise (PSE). I highly recommend the PSE to better understand your motives: http://www .haygroup.com/leadershipandtalentondemand/ourproducts/item _details.aspx?itemid=53&type=7.

203 **the affiliation motive:** Hay Group has conducted quite a bit of research in this area. For more information, go to http://www.haygroup.com and look under Picture Story Exercise (PSE).

203 **apply to your work:** Picture Story Exercise (PSE): https://www .haygroup.com/leadershipandtalentondemand/ourproducts/item _details.aspx?itemid=53&type=7&t=2; Personal Values Questionnaire (PVQ): https://www.haygroup.com/leadershipandtalentondemand/our products/item_details.aspx?itemid=38&type=7&t=2.

204 **sign up for.":** Mark Blecher, in an interview with the author, January 2016.

208 **"career best" experiences:** Kurt Sandholtz, "Achieving Your Career Best," *National Business Employment Weekly*, July 11–17, 1999.

8. You Can't Count on "The Man"

211 **your best customers:** Stephen R. Covey, *The 7 Habits of Highly Effective Families* (New York: St. Martin's Press, 2014).

211 **development store yet.":** Michael M. Lombardo and Robert W. Eichinger, *The Leadership Machine* (Minneapolis, MN: Lominger Limited, 2005), 34.

213 **to their employees:** Elizabeth G. Chambers, Mark Foulon, Helen Handfield-Jones, Steven M. Hankin, and Edward G. Michaels, "The War for Talent," *McKinsey Quarterly* (1998): 44–57.

213 **performance problems.":** Michael M. Lombardo and Robert W. Eichinger, *The Career Architect Development Planner* (Minneapolis, MN: Lominger Limited, 1996), 19, 120.

214 **feedback all the time.":** Greg Welch, in an interview with the author, November 2015.

214 **strokes gained in putting:** http://www.golfdigest.com/story/rory-mcilroy -hires-putting-coach-to-help-stanch-the-bleeding.

214 **each and every week.":** Ibid.

214 **I use it frequently.":** Craig Wortmann, in an interview with the author, November 2016.

215 **explicit gender bias:** Recommended reading includes: Mahzarin R. Banaji and Anthony G. Greenwald, *Blindspot: Hidden Biases of Good People* (New York: Bantam Books, 2013); Herminia Ibarra, Robin Ely, and Deborah Kolb, "Women Rising: The Unseen Barriers," *Harvard Business Review* 91, no. 9 (2013): 60–66; and Anne-Marie Slaughter, "Why Women Still Can't Have It All," *The Atlantic*, July /August 2012, http://www.theatlantic.com/magazine/archive/2012/07 /why-women-still-cant-have-it-all/309020/.

215 **become more assertive.":** Candice Frankovelgia, in an interview with the author, March 2015.

215 **leadership and as executives:** Books such as Sheryl Sandberg, *Lean In: Women, Work, and the Will to Lead* (New York: Random House, 2013); Katty Kay and Claire Shipman, *The Confidence Code* (New York: Harper Business, 2014); and Joanna Barsh, Susie Cranston, and Geoffrey Lewis, *How Remarkable Women Lead: The Breakthrough Model for Work and Life* (New York: Crown Business, 2011).

215 **chip away at for decades.":** Betsy Holden, in an interview with the author, July 2016.

216 **internal mentors:** Boris Groysberg, "How Star Women Build Portable Skills," *Harvard Business Review* 86, no. 2 (2008): 74.

216 **male-dominated firm.":** Ibid.

216 **internal relationships.":** Ibid.

217 **No one else will.'":** Betsy Holden, in an interview with the author, July 2016.

218 **"ask for the sale."**: Ibarra, Ely, and Kolb, "Women Rising."

218 **rather than rewarded:** Ibid.

218 **networks for women:** https://leanin.org/

224 **let me do my job?'"**: Suein L. Hwang, "Dot-Com Blur: Venture Capitalists Discover the Weight of Marketing," *Wall Street Journal*, February 16, 2000, https://www.wsj.com/articles/SB950660543896923766.

228 **win support for change."**: Kerry A. Bunker, Kathy E. Kram, and Sharon Ting, "The Young and the Clueless," *Harvard Business Review* 80, no. 12 (2002): 80–87.

228 **and leadership skills:** Morgan W. McCall, *High Flyers: Developing the Next Generation of Leaders* (Boston: Harvard Business Press, 1998), 53–56.

228 **three fundamental areas:** In *High Flyers*, Morgan McCall goes into more detail on the ways that organizations can improve their development efforts with talented managers.

229 **those employees' salaries:** William Gentry, Scott Mondore, and Brennan Cox, "A Study of Managerial Derailment Characteristics and Personality Preferences," *Journal of Management Development* 26, no. 9 (2007): 857; Bradford Smart and Geoff Smart, *Topgrading: How Leading Companies Win by Hiring, Coaching and Keeping the Best People* (New York: Penguin Books, 2005) 36–55; Susan J. Wells, "Diving In," *HR Magazine* 50, no. 3 (2005), 1–2.

230 **likelihood of derailment:** William Gentry and Linda Rhoades Shanock, "Views of Managerial Derailment from Above and Below," *Journal of Applied Social Psychology* 38, no. 10 (2008): 2469. Erik De Haan and Anthony Kasozi, *The Leadership Shadow: How to Recognize and Avoid Derailment, Hubris and Overdrive* (London: Kogan Page, 2014), 7–13.

230 **that might afflict you:** Michael M. Lombardo and Robert W. Eichinger, *The Career Architect Development Planner* (Minneapolis, MN: Lominger Limited, 2006), vi.

232 **at my wit's end."**: I changed the subject's name to protect his anonymity.

236 **as well as their strengths:** Guangrong Dai, Maynard Goff, Joy Hazucha, and James Lewis, "Detecting Derailers," Korn Ferry Institute, 2014, 3,

http://www.hrpulse.co.za/downloads/Korn-Ferry-Institute-Detecting
-derailers.pdf.

236 "in a persistent state of beta,": LinkedIn founder Reid Hoffman uses
that term in his book with Ben Casnocha, *The Startup of You* (New
York: Crown Business, 2012).

ACKNOWLEDGMENTS

I thought it would be hard to write a book, and it was harder than I thought. Thankfully, I had a lot of help.

Thank you, Adam Grant, for epitomizing the traits you espoused in *Give and Take*—providing me with your perspective on the positioning of this book and for sending me several spot-on research studies and articles. Also, thank you for introducing me to my agent, Giles Anderson.

Thank you, Giles, for helping to create a book proposal that enabled us to land the PublicAffairs imprint within the Hachette/Perseus Book Group and, in particular, John Mahaney as the editor.

John Mahaney: thank you for your tremendous dedication and rigor in editing this book. While there were times I felt I would buckle under the weight of your high standard, that standard made this book *vastly* better.

To Michael Meier, thank you so much for developing the ingenious illustrations in the book. They help set the tone of the book. On top of that, you were such a pleasure to work with.

Thank you, Dean Sally Blount, for your ongoing support during my time at Kellogg. You've not only provided me with the resources to dive into the research of career derailment, but, more importantly, you've been a valued mentor to me.

And thank you, Brooke Vuckovic, for your wise counsel and encouragement throughout the past three years of this project.

You've helped me in so many areas that it's nearly impossible to itemize them. I owe you, big time. Maybe a trip to Miraval Resort & Spa?

I have also relied on the good judgment of my Kellogg partner, Paul Corona, the director of Full-Time MBA Leadership Development, in advising me on this book. Thank you, Paul, for your support and perspective.

Thank you, Marshall Goldsmith, for your scholarship on this topic as well as your generosity—you have provided your support every step of the way.

Thank you, Florian Schafer, for your selflessness in helping with my research and to Deloitte Consulting LLP for offering their resources. I'd also like to thank you, Sara Dreyfuss, for your assistance in conducting my literature review in the early stages of my research.

Thank you, Dan Pink, for taking several calls and e-mails from me, a complete stranger, and advising me on the complexities of writing a book. I kept your advice in mind as I plugged away, year after year. P.S. Go 'Cats!

I am so appreciative of all the people who allowed me to interview them on the hard-to-discuss topic of career derailment. For purposes of anonymity I won't list all their names, but I am appreciative, in particular, of the time and insight the following people generously offered me. They are, in no particular order: Brock Leach, Laila Tarraf, Harry Kraemer, Leigh Thompson, Matt McCall, Laura Flanagan, Geoff Smart, Stuart Kaplan, Dan Marriott, John Pleasants, Betsy Holden, Doug Kush, Jana Rich, Raul Vazquez, Kevin Murnane, Ted Martin, Greg Welch, Alex Moy, Guangrong Dai, Ruth Malloy, Smruti Rajagopalan, Tod Francis, Eric Lauterbach, Dick Costolo, Tina James, Mike Gamson, Ana Dutra, Tim Simonds, Betsy Ziegler, Craig Wortmann, Chip Conley, Jon Morris, Mike Luecht, Mike Hogan, Mark Blecher, Liza

Kirkpatrick, Mary Simon, Matthew Temple, Jay Fehnel, and Gary Briggs. I'm sure I missed a few people and for that I apologize in advance!

I would like to recognize the academic research that was the foundation of this book. In particular, I relied on the insightful work of Robert and Joyce Hogan, the research team at the Center for Creative Leadership, who blazed a trail on this topic years ago, Michael Lombardo, Richard Eichinger, Morgan McCall, Robert Kaiser, Robert Kaplan, Marshall Goldsmith, William Gentry, George Hollenbeck, John Zenger, Joseph Folkman, David Dotlich, Peter Cairo, Linda Hill, Sydney Finkelstein, the Korn Ferry Institute (and Guangrong Dai, in particular), the research of Hay Group, Jean Brittain Leslie, Ellen Van Velsor, David McClelland, Dan Pink, Daniel Goleman, and the person many credit for pioneering the work on the topic of managerial derailment, V. J. Bentz. This is certainly not a complete list—to the many I didn't mention, whose derailment research moved the ball forward, I apologize.

I've been very lucky to have had some great bosses and role models over my thirty years in business. Several have gotten me out of hot water (uh, you out there, Stephen?). I owe a big debt of gratitude to Larry Cates, Bob Brent, Stephen Quinn, Brock Leach, Mike Weaver, Mick Parrott, Jeanne Jackson, John Fleming, Sally Blount, Chris Girgenti, and J. B. Pritzker. I clearly wouldn't have progressed very far in my career without them. And thank you, Mike Hogan, for the strong cup of coffee when I was drowsy at the wheel in 1995. Also, I'd like to offer a special thanks to Gill Butler, the towering figure who inspired me in my formative years at PepsiCo.

Thank you, Mom, Dad, Meg, and Jen for your encouragement of this venture. Regardless of the topic, from writing this book to becoming a teacher (or, going way back—competitive swimming), you've always been supportive, which has given me the confidence to attempt things that, for me, had a high degree of difficulty.

Finally, I would like to thank my wife, partner, and the great love of my life, Allyson, for her love, unswerving support, and encouragement of this book project ("Keep going, P—you're over halfway done!") and for being so understanding when I had to disappear for stretches of time to hole up and write.

Oh—one last thing—I'm giving the goofy smile face to Glen, Sammy, and Claire right now.

Carter Cast, a professor at Northwestern University's Kellogg School of Management, was selected by his students six years running to receive the Faculty Impact Award. When not teaching, Cast is a venture partner at Pritzker Group Venture Capital, where he invests in early-stage technology companies such as the Dollar Shave Club and SMS Assist, Inc. He is a lead mentor for TechStars Chicago, one of the country's leading technology start-up accelerators, and has been featured in "The Accelerators," a *Wall Street Journal* forum in which start-up mentors discuss strategies for and challenges of creating a new business. Cast's writings have appeared in the *Wall Street Journal* and *New York Times*. He has been a guest on shows on Bloomberg, CNN, CNBC, and Fox. Prior to his academic and venture capital career, Cast was the chief executive officer at Walmart.com. During his tenure, Walmart.com became the third-highest-volume e-commerce company, behind Amazon and eBay. Before his career at Walmart, Cast was an officer and part of the launch team for Blue Nile Inc., the leading online diamond and jewelry retailer. Prior to that, he was vice president of product marketing for Electronic Arts, launching products such as *The Sims*. Cast started his career at PepsiCo, where he derailed early on before recovering to become director of marketing in the Frito-Lay division.

PublicAffairs is a publishing house founded in 1997. It is a tribute to the standards, values, and flair of three persons who have served as mentors to countless reporters, writers, editors, and book people of all kinds, including me.

I. F. STONE, proprietor of *I. F. Stone's Weekly*, combined a commitment to the First Amendment with entrepreneurial zeal and reporting skill and became one of the great independent journalists in American history. At the age of eighty, Izzy published *The Trial of Socrates*, which was a national bestseller. He wrote the book after he taught himself ancient Greek.

BENJAMIN C. BRADLEE was for nearly thirty years the charismatic editorial leader of *The Washington Post*. It was Ben who gave the *Post* the range and courage to pursue such historic issues as Watergate. He supported his reporters with a tenacity that made them fearless and it is no accident that so many became authors of influential, best-selling books.

ROBERT L. BERNSTEIN, the chief executive of Random House for more than a quarter century, guided one of the nation's premier publishing houses. Bob was personally responsible for many books of political dissent and argument that challenged tyranny around the globe. He is also the founder and longtime chair of Human Rights Watch, one of the most respected human rights organizations in the world.

. . .

For fifty years, the banner of Public Affairs Press was carried by its owner Morris B. Schnapper, who published Gandhi, Nasser, Toynbee, Truman, and about 1,500 other authors. In 1983, Schnapper was described by *The Washington Post* as "a redoubtable gadfly." His legacy will endure in the books to come.

Peter Osnos, *Founder*